A SOUTHERN-STYLE CHRISTMAS

A
Southern-Style
CHRISTMAS

Holiday Treasures from

JAN KARON ❧ MAX LUCADO ❧ LIZ CURTIS HIGGS

MICHAEL CARD ❧ RUTH BELL GRAHAM ❧ AND OTHERS

COMPILED BY LUCINDA SECREST MCDOWELL

 **SHAW**

A Southern-Style Christmas
A SHAW BOOK
PUBLISHED BY WATERBROOK PRESS
2375 Telstar Drive, Suite 160
Colorado Springs, CO 80920
A division of Random House, Inc.

Unless otherwise noted all Scripture quotations are taken from the HOLY BIBLE, NEW INTERNATIONAL VERSION®. NIV®. Copyright © 1973, 1978, 1984 International Bible Society. Used by permission of Zondervan Publishing House. All rights reserved. The "NIV" and "New International Version" trademarks are registered in the United States Patent and Trademark Office by International Bible Society. Use of either trademark requires permission of International Bible Society.

All acknowledgments are listed on pages 126–127.

ISBN 0-87788-781-0

Interior design by Tobias Design

Interior photographs © PhotoDisc

Library of Congress Cataloging-in-Publication Data

A southern style Christmas / compiled by Lucinda Secrest McDowell:
holiday treasures from Jan Karon, Max Lucado . . . [et al.].
  p. cm.
  ISBN 0-87788-781-0 (cloth)
  1. Christmas—Southern States. 2. Southern States—Social life and
customs. I. McDowell, Lucinda Secrest, 1953- II. Marshall, Catherine.

GT4989.A2 S687 2000
394.2663'0975—dc21   00-030587

Printed in the USA
02 01 00 / 3 2 1

For my sisters
Cathy Secrest Ray and Susan Secrest Waters
with whom I shared the joy and wonder
of many southern Christmases

Contents

Section III: "It was again Christmas in the Old South."

SECTION IV: "Christmas was really just a time for everybody getting together."

SECTION V: "It was my most memorable Christmas."

Section VI: "What if Christmas were both a beginning and an end?"

What makes Christmas special?

When you reflect upon that question, chances are your mind naturally returns to the Christmases of your childhood. For me, those celebrations of Jesus' birth took place in the town of Thomasville, Georgia, where my extended family still lives today. Now I rarely have the opportunity to spend the holidays there. But with every whiff of sweet potato pie, every sound of Elvis Presley's "I'll Be Home for Christmas," and every sight of a live nativity scene near a church, I am transported back to that time and place.

There is no *one* southern Christmas experience because this region varies dramatically in culture, climate, and celebration. Yet our similarities are far greater than our differences. For both native-born and adopted southerners, Christmas is primarily a season of generosity, hospitality, and faith. Most of all it is an opportunity to celebrate the people who touch our lives each day.

This book celebrates Christmas as seen through the eyes of people whose roots and hearts are deep in the South. While we in the twenty-first century have increasingly become "citizens of the world," it is the wise person who is able to keep up with the times while still retaining that most important part of home and heritage—a tough balance, but well worth it.

So whatever your background and memories, I invite you to listen to the stories, savor the recipes, sing the carols, and soak up the beauty of Christmas with me—a Southern-Style Christmas.

—LUCINDA SECREST MCDOWELL

Christmas in the South

It's Christmas and the sky is bright,
There is no chance of snow tonight.
We children play outside all day,
But never have we seen a sleigh
  AT CHRISTMAS IN THE SOUTH.

Our family comes from far and near
With lots of yummy food to share.
There's cornbread stuffing and sweet potato pie,
Mamalu's eggnog and ham piled high
  FOR CHRISTMAS IN THE SOUTH.

The churches fill with songs of joy
Celebrating Mary's baby boy.
And towns can still display those mangers
Without the ridicule of strangers
  ON CHRISTMAS IN THE SOUTH.

We snuggle by the fire's glow
With air conditioners turned down low;
While sipping on hot chocolate,
And dreaming of the toys we'll get
  THIS CHRISTMAS IN THE SOUTH.

I've lived a lot of places since I was a little girl,
And Christmased in some fascinating corners of the world.
From Boston to Chicago and the San Francisco Bay,
From Seattle to New England which is where I live today.
And I know that what's important is my faith and family,
Which means that I can celebrate wherever I may be.
But my roots are deep, my memories clear,
And I feel a longing every year
  TO CHRISTMAS IN THE SOUTH.

—LUCINDA SECREST MCDOWELL

SECTION I

"Christmas begins with a Baby."

How to Keep Your
Christmas Joy

CHARLES L. ALLEN, *Georgia*

My father used to have the most wonderful garden each year, and we always had fresh vegetables in great abundance. Mother, looking ahead to the cold winter days when the garden would be covered by dead leaves, spent many hours canning the beans, tomatoes, and other good things. Then in the months that followed she would go to the pantry and take the jars from the shelves. She made it possible for us to have vegetables all year round.

Could we do something like that with the wonderful Christmas spirit? Perhaps we could store up the good feeling we have at Christmas and let a little of it loose in our lives on each of the days that follow. Let us see how it may be possible.

Christmas begins with a Baby. As long as babies are born, the world has hope. Consider the year 1809, for example. It was a bleak and dismal time. A ruthless dictator seemed certain to conquer the world, and there was almost no hope left in anyone's heart. One morning in February of that year a traveler walked into a country store in the mountains of Kentucky. He asked, "Anything new happen around here lately?" "Nothing ever happens around here," someone replied. "There was a baby born up at the Lincoln cabin last night— that's all." That was one of the most important things that ever happened in this great country of ours. In that year other babies were born: Charles Darwin and Gladstone, Tennyson and Edgar Allan Poe, Cyrus McCormick and Mendelssohn. You never know what may happen in the world because a baby has been born.

At Christmas our pulses beat more quickly because we know the coming of that Baby has done more to soften the hardness of the world's heart, to bring hope in the midst of the world's despair, and to bring joy in the midst of sadness, than any event that has ever taken place since the beginning of time. As we consider Him, our own hearts are softened and our lives are transformed. I wish we might think about that Baby every day of the year; in that way we shall keep our Christmas joy.

The Bible says, "In him was life." We use the word *life* to describe so many things that we become confused concerning what life really is. So, when John said, "In him was life," just what was he talking about? If we might know, then we would surely know a Christmas joy that can be cherished all year round.

How can we keep our Christmas joy all the year? Loving service to others is part of the answer. But to all of this must be added something more. At Christmastime we long to be close to Christ. We are ashamed of our wrongs, and we are inspired to change. When we do what we should, marvelous power and peace come into our lives, and our troubles seem to vanish. We need to be close to Christ, not only at Christmas, but throughout the year. Then the joy of Christmas will continue in our hearts.

Mary Had a Baby

*A popular theme in African-American Christmas carols
centered around the fragile image of the young woman Mary
with her helpless infant—the Christ child. This spiritual was
probably created in the nineteenth century, possibly in South Carolina.*

Mary had a baby, Oh Lord;
Mary had a baby, Oh my Lord;
Mary had a baby, Oh Lord;
The people keep a-coming and the train done gone.

What did she name Him? Oh Lord;
What did she name Him? Oh my Lord;
What did she name Him? Oh Lord;
The people keep a-coming and the train done gone.

She called Him Jesus, Oh Lord;
She called Him Jesus, Oh my Lord;
She called Him Jesus, Oh Lord;
The people keep a-coming and the train done gone.

Where was He born? Oh Lord;
Where was He born? Oh my Lord;
Where was He born? Oh Lord;
The people keep a-coming and the train done gone.

Born in a stable, Oh Lord;
Born in a stable, Oh my Lord;
Born in a stable, Oh Lord;
The people keep a-coming and the train done gone.

Where did they lay Him? Oh Lord;
Where did they lay Him? Oh my Lord;
Where did they lay Him? Oh Lord;
The people keep a-coming and the train done gone.

Laid Him in a manger, Oh Lord;
Laid Him in a manger, Oh my Lord;
Laid Him in a manger, Oh Lord;
The people keep a-coming and the train done gone.

A Christmas Verse

PRATT SECREST, *Georgia*

Our Lord Jesus looked down upon the earth
  To watch us in worship rejoice in His birth!
And to listen again to the stories of old
  Of His coming to earth as the angels foretold.
Oh wonder of wonders that God sent His Son
  To offer salvation to everyone!
The centuries have come and the centuries have gone
  And His promise is fresh, ev'ry night, ev'ry morn.

We celebrate Christmas with laughter and mirth
  And in reverence, we pause to give thanks for His birth.
So let the bells chime, let laughter ring out
  "His Kingdom's forever!" we sing and we shout.
But may we remember the race is not won
  Until *all* men give praise to God's only Son!
He offers grace and salvation from sin
  To *all* who will welcome and let Him come in.
He may come to *you* as a man or a child . . .
  In a storm or a sunset . . . or a whisper so mild.
But know He is with you when each day is done
  He's always with you . . . He's God's blessed Son!

A Fresh Approach to the Holidays

ANN HIBBARD, *Virginia*

Most people fondly dream of a "Currier and Ives" Christmas, complete with blazing fires and Christmas carols sung around a tinsel-draped tree with a loving, harmonious family. For many, however, Christmas serves as a stark reminder of family tensions, grief, and broken relationships. Christmas cheer gives way to dashed hopes and holiday depression.

Many of us simply dread Christmas because of all the work. How in the world can we fit Christmas card-writing, baking, and endless hours of shopping into already packed schedules? Why can't Christmas be the season of peace and joy that we crave? No matter what your situation, there is hope. This Christmas can be the most meaningful Christmas of your life. Here are some practical steps that have helped me to change the tone of my Christmas.

Step One: Adopt Realistic Expectations

Most of the pressure we feel at Christmas can be attributed to expectations—preconceived ideas of what Christmas should be. These pressures come from our culture, from our family members, and from within ourselves.

Where (and with whom) will we celebrate Christmas? For whom do we buy gifts? How much do we spend? What about Santa Claus? What kind of tree? What do we eat on Christmas Eve or Christmas Day? We all have differing expectations based on previous experience and current convictions.

As if this weren't bad enough, often our own expectations and those forced on us by others don't match. Those of us who like to "please everyone" find ourselves squeezed in an emotional vise. It is simply impossible to make everyone happy—nor should this be our goal.

Admit Our Limitations

In order to free ourselves from the bondage of all these expectations, we first need to admit that we cannot do it all. We simply cannot be everything to everyone. We need to take a good look at our own limitations. Each of us has limited time, energy, abilities, and resources. Because we are finite, we need to make choices—what we will and will not do. I needed to admit that making twelve kinds of Christmas cookies (like my mother had done) was no longer a priority for me.

Agree on a Realistic Plan

Once we admit our limitations, we need to agree on a realistic plan for Christmas. This means sitting down with your family, particularly your spouse if you are married, and discussing your hopes for your Christmas season. If your children are old enough, include them in the discussion. Find out what is important to each person in terms of celebrating Christmas. What traditions does each one cherish? What activities are important for the family to attend? Have your calendar handy so that you can mark out the times and dates to do those special things.

Accept What We Cannot Change

Ask yourself, does the success of my Christmas depend on someone else's behavior? Often family dynamics at holidays are like a pressure cooker ready to explode. Chances are, people will behave badly. The patterns that our relationships fall into normally are just as prevalent at Christmas—if not more so. Remember: You are not responsible for others' behavior—only your own. If you can realistically accept the givens in your situation, you will be less anxious and more at liberty to make a positive difference.

Step Two: Put Aside Resentment

The second step to a happier Christmas is to put aside resentment. Underlying anger saps our energy and chokes our joy. If that person who continues to hurt or annoy you never changes, what will you do? Holding on to resentment turns us into bitter, negative people. I for one do not want to turn into such a person. But is there an alternative?

Someone has said that "to forgive is to set the prisoner free only to discover that the prisoner was you." Christmas is a wonderful time to begin to forgive those who have hurt or disappointed you. After all, the reason Jesus Christ came to earth was to bring forgiveness for our sins and restoration to our broken relationship with God. And he will give us the power to forgive others if we have given our lives to him and are seeking to love and obey him.

Step Three: Change What You Can

Once you have accepted the reality of your situation and put aside resentment, you need to determine what you can do to make your Christmas better. Here are some suggestions for relieving the pressure so that you can be at your best.

Physical

When Elijah was exhausted after his showdown with the prophets of Baal on Mt. Carmel, he became depressed to the point of wanting to die. God sent his angel to minister to Elijah in the desert, and the first order of business was food and rest (1 Kings 19). Physical depletion quickly translates into emotional and spiritual depression. In order to be at our best for the Christmas season, we need to take care of ourselves physically. Getting enough sleep should be a priority. Rest does wonders for a person's temper as well as one's perspective.

Emotional

Essential to maintaining emotional equilibrium during the Christmas season is to plan a sane schedule. Write out a list of the things that you need to do, and then get your calendar and plan when you will do them. Often tasks don't seem quite so daunting when they are broken down into bite-sized pieces.

I must confess that I am easily overwhelmed by a busy schedule. If I have one obligation on my calendar per day for a week, I experience a panic attack! Most people can handle more activities than I can. You need to know your own threshold and the kind of pace that your family can handle comfortably.

Allow me to put in one word of caution here, however: If we are always on the run, we miss hearing some important voices. We can miss hearing our children's voices—they see that we are too busy, so they don't share what is troubling them. We can miss hearing our spouse's voice, for we never have a chance to talk. Most important, we miss hearing God's voice. Slow down enough so that you can hear voices this Christmas.

Perhaps the best thing we can do to strengthen ourselves emotionally is to reach out to others during this season. One year, we called our local hospice and arranged to bring cards to the patients there. Another year we bought Christmas presents for a needy family in the inner city. Experiences such as these put everything into perspective. Greed and self-centeredness come so naturally to all of us. Making these small sacrifices of time and energy to help the needy really helps us most of all. We get our focus off ourselves. Our own problems suddenly seem smaller. And the lessons our children learn are invaluable.

Spiritual

The most significant realm of our lives is the spiritual, which permeates everything we are. We cannot afford to neglect the spiritual, if we want to have a happy and meaningful Christmas.

First, we need to seek an eternal perspective. It helps to ask yourself, "What is really important?" According to the Bible, there are only two things on earth that are eternal: God's Word and people's souls. Remembering this truth helps me to keep my priorities in line.

Second, we need to draw near to God during this holy season. Four Sundays before Christmas begins the season of Advent, or "coming." Advent is a time of reflection and repentance. It helps us to prepare our hearts for the celebration of Christ's birth.

For my family, Advent has become a wonderful time of growth. Each evening we gather around the lighted Advent candles, read and discuss verses that point to Christ's coming, and sing a beloved Christmas carol. These moments of quiet worship and reflection instill in us a sense of peace that we carry with us throughout the month. More than that, as we meet Christ together each day, Jesus becomes the focus of our Christmas.

Take time out each day to meet Christ one-on-one, as well. It helps me to remember that this is the most important thing I do each day. Only in Christ do I find the strength to meet the tasks and challenges of the day. Jesus Christ gives me purpose, perspective, and peace. When I find that I have become short-tempered with my family, ungrateful in my attitudes, or preoccupied with the unimportant, it is usually because I have been neglecting my relationship with the Lord. If I am growing in that all-important relationship, my other relationships seem to fall into place.

Perhaps this idea of a "relationship with Christ" is new to you. Take an honest look deep within you. Is there something missing? There is an emptiness within each of us that can only be filled with God himself. He made us to know him, and until we know him, we are incomplete. Advent is a perfect time to begin to get to know Jesus Christ. God says, "You will seek me and find me when you seek me with all your heart" (Jeremiah 29:13).

I Wonder As I Wander

APPALACHIAN CAROL

I wonder as I wander out under the sky,
How Jesus, the Savior, did come forth to die;
For poor, ornery people like you and like I—
I wonder as I wander,

Out under the sky.

When Mary birthed Jesus, 'twas in a cow's stall,
With wise men and farmers and shepherds and all.
But high from God's heaven a star's light did fall,
And the promise of ages

It then did recall.

If Jesus had wanted for any wee thing,
A star in the sky or a bird on the wing;
Or all of God's angels in heaven to sing,
He surely could have had it,

'Cause He was the King!

I wonder as I wander out under the sky,
How Jesus, the Savior, did come forth to die;
For poor, ornery people like you and like I—
I wonder as I wander,

Out under the sky.

SECTION II

"It's no gift if it's something you didn't care about."

There's No Such Thing As a Poor Christmas

C E L E S T I N E   S I B L E Y, *Georgia*

My mother, Muv, once made dumplings to go with three cans of Vienna sausage for Thanksgiving dinner.

If you've ever bought Vienna sausage for seven cents a can at a sawmill-turpentine still commissary, you will understand the significance of that.

It bespeaks a woman of imagination. Who else would think the union of Vienna sausage and dumplings possible, much less feasible?

More important, it indicates an unquenchable zest for celebration.

Muv believes that you should put everything you have and everything you can get into an important occasion. We *had* the Vienna sausage—and very little else in those Depression years of the 1930s. She made the dumplings.

When I think of that Thanksgiving dinner, served out of the Sunday dishes, on the very best tablecloth, with a fire burning brightly on the hearth and a bowlful of apples our cousin sent from Virginia polished to a high sheen for a centerpiece, I wouldn't dare question Muv's convictions about Christmas.

For if Thanksgiving is important—and oh, it is!—how much more important is Christmas. Anybody who would po'mouth Christmas, contends my mother, is guilty of sinning against both heaven and his fellow man. He's a hangdog, mean-spirited character who is unworthy of receiving the greatest Gift of all time.

My father, reared a Scotch Presbyterian with a more moderate (Muv would say tepid) approach to most things, may have once regarded Muv's feelings about Christmas as a bit extravagant. But early in their marriage she beat him into line with weapons he normally handled best—ethical and spiritual arguments.

He made the mistake one grayish December morning of observing bleakly that the lumber business was going badly and "it looks like a poor Christmas this year."

"A *poor* Christmas!" cried Muv. "Shame on you! There's no such thing as a poor Christmas!"

Poor people and hard times, yes. They were not new in Christ's time, and they were certainly not new in rural Alabama. But no matter what you had or didn't have in a material way, Christmas stood by itself—glorious and unmatched by anything else that had happened in the history of the world. Jesus himself had come to dwell among men, and with a richness like that to celebrate, who could be so meaching and self-centered as to speak of a "poor" Christmas?

"Make a joyful noise unto the Lord!" directed Muv gustily, and if my father found he couldn't do that, he at least didn't grouse. He was to learn later that he didn't dare to even *look* unjoyful about the approach of Christmas, or Muv would do something wild and unprecedented to cheer him up, like the year she took tailoring lessons and made him a new suit and topped it off by buying him a pearl stickpin at a $1-down-and-charge jewelry store.

The suit was beautifully made and a perfect fit, and Muv had even worked out the cost of the goods by helping the tailor, but I think it made my father a little uneasy to be so splendidly arrayed at a time when he had come to accept, even to take pride in, the image of himself as a "poor man." And the idea of *owing* for something as frivolous as a piece of jewelry was so repugnant to him that he finished paying for the stickpin himself. But he loved having it, wore it with pleasure, and thereafter looked at Muv and the ardor which she poured into preparations for Christmas with a touch of awe.

"Things aren't important. People are," Muv preached, and it sounded so fine it was years before I realized what she meant to *us*. Things weren't important to us, so as fast as gift packages came in from distant kin, Muv unwrapped them, admired them and with a gleam in her eye that I came to dread said happily, "Now *who* can we give this to?"

It's funny that with the passage of the years only one or two of the Things stand out in memory. There were some lavender garters a boy in the sixth grade gave me.

("Beautiful!" said Muv. "You can give them to Aunt Sister!") And there was a green crepe de chine dress I think I still mourn for a little bit. ("Oh, it's so pretty! Don't you want to give it to Julia Belle?")

Julia Belle was a skinny little Negro girl in the quarters who had lost her baby in a fire and kept wandering up and down the road wringing her hands and crying. My green dress was such a dazzling gift, it did divert her from her grief a little, and it may have helped her along the road to recovery.

At the time, I remember protesting that I loved the dress and wanted it myself and Muv said blithely, "Of course you do. It's no gift if it's something you don't care about!"

It must be true because the other Things are lost to memory, but the People remain. Through the years there have been a lot of them, disreputable, distinguished, outrageous, inspiring, and at Christmastime I remember them and the gifts they gave to me—the gifts, in fact, that they *were*.

The Perfect Christmas Present

LUCINDA SECREST McDOWELL,
Georgia

"Thanks be to God for His
indescribable gift."

— 2 CORINTHIANS 9:15

There is one Christmas Day incident from years ago when we lived in North Carolina that I'd rather forget. At least I'm ashamed at the immature and self-centered way I handled it. You see, after much thought and sacrificial financial investment, I gave someone what I believed to be the Perfect Christmas Present. And that person didn't like it.

Well, at least the friend didn't respond in the glowing appreciative manner I had envisioned. In my disappointment I'm afraid I sulked, hosted a self-pity party, and vowed to give that person just a brown paper bag next year. "Who needs gift-giving, anyway?" I muttered.

Who indeed?

God, the One who started the whole thing, after all, by sending His only Son as a Gift to us at Christmas, decided to teach me a few things. He reminded me that the very essence of a gift is that the giver wants to bestow it on someone with no strings attached. No promise to use it or wear it or play it; no reciprocal gift; and no obligatory thank-you note of appreciation. In other words, it's *free*!

Can I truly give like that this Christmas? Can you?

The good news is that while our gift-giving shouldn't be contingent on a favorable response or appreciation, much of the time people do express their thanks. But that's just the icing on the cake. John 3:16 reminds us that "God loved us so much that He gave His Son." James 1:17 says that "every good and perfect gift is from above."

Rather than focusing on whether or not others have thanked us for our gifts, maybe it's time to do a personal spiritual inventory. What are some of the gifts I've received from God this year? Have I thanked Him lately?

He didn't give because He expects or needs my appreciation. He gave because He *loves* me!

I think I'll thank Him anyway.

SUGARED PECANS

We had a beautiful grove of pecan trees on our farm, and some of my fondest childhood memories are of shooting the clumps of mistletoe down from the branches of the pecan trees where they gathered. We all hoped that someone special would kiss us under the mistletoe. These sugared pecans make a great gift wrapped in festive bags and bows. L. S. M.

2 cups pecan halves

1 cup sugar

1 tablespoon butter

1/2 cup milk

1/2 teaspoon salt

Set pecans aside. Cook all other ingredients until a drop of the mixture forms a soft ball in cold water. Now add pecans to the mixture and cook until it begins to granulate (takes about 5 minutes). Spoon mixture onto a buttered plate until it hardens, and then break into pieces.

CRANBERRY BREAD

MINLU CHASTAIN HASTY, *Georgia*

Homemade sweet bread—nothing better to share with neighbors and friends.
This recipe from my grandmother was always a favorite at Christmas. L. S. M.

Sift together twice the following:

2 cups flour

1 1/2 teaspoons baking powder

1 cup sugar

1/2 teaspoon salt

1/2 teaspoon soda

To the juice and grated rind of 1 orange, add 2 tablespoons shortening (Crisco) and enough boiling water to make 3/4 cup. Add to this liquid 1 beaten egg, and then add the liquid mixture to all the dry ingredients. Stir in 1 cup chopped nuts and 1 cup raw cranberries, cut in half. Pour in well-greased loaf pan and bake 1 1/4 hours at 325 degrees.

Note: It slices better if kept in refrigerator.

Blue Jeans and Jesus

SHARRON McDONALD, *Arkansas*

I'll always remember the winter when I was six years old. It was very cold in our poor country town in southern Arkansas, and my sister and I walked the two miles to school that year. The teacher was always glad to see us, and sympathetic when we arrived half frozen. We wore just the barest of clothing: worn-out underwear and shoes, and ill-fitting cotton dresses. It was all we had.

One day the class had a Christmas party, but my sister and I didn't have a present to bring. We just sat back and watched. We were given little paper cups filled with candy, which we ate right then and there. Then the teacher brought us a present, and it was big! We wanted to admire it for a while, but the teacher said to open it.

Inside were two brand-new pairs of blue jeans! When we put them on, we felt so grown up. The teacher hugged us and said, "I just wanted to say I love you, and Jesus loves you, too."

Walking the two miles home that day, we walked a little taller and straighter, and the wind seemed less cold.

Each Christmas, I now hang denim stockings as a reminder of that year. I'll never forget that my teacher and Jesus loved me.

Nu Nu's Hot Chocolate Mix

CAROL HASTY SINGLETERY, *Georgia*

Jars of homemade hot chocolate mix make a great gift, and this recipe of my Aunt Carol's is a tested favorite. Just remember to save lots of used pickle jars and large baby food jars during the year. Use pinking shears to cut a calico circle for a festive lid cover. Include a card with the recipe and your Christmas greetings. L. S. M.

4 1/2 cups (1 lb.) of Nestle's Quik

1 8-quart box of powdered milk

2/3 cup of powdered sugar
(more or less to suit your taste)

1 11-oz. jar of Coffeemate creamer

Stir together and store in large container. Use 1/3 cup mix to each cup of hot water. Yields 48 cups.

Savory Spiced Tea

Here is another gift idea for those empty jars you've been collecting. This instant tea is great for a cozy evening by the fire. Don't forget to attach a card with the recipe and measuring instructions. Enjoy! L. S. M.

2 cups instant orange drink mix *(like Tang)*

1 cup instant tea mix *(I use decaffeinated.)*

1 10-oz. box of instant lemonade mix

1 to 1 1/2 cups sugar

2 teaspoons cinnamon

1 teaspoon ground allspice

1 teaspoon ground cloves

Mix all ingredients together. Store in a tightly closed jar. Use 2 teaspoons per cup of hot water.

A Mitford Christmas

JAN KARON, *North Carolina*

According to parishioners, the Christmas Eve masses at Lord's Chapel were more beautiful, more powerful, more stirring than ever before.

Candles burned on the window sills, among fragrant boughs of spruce and pine. Fresh garlands wrapped the high cedar beams over the nave. A glorious tree from Meadowgate Farm stood near the pulpit, and a lush garden of creme-colored poinsettias sprang up around its feet. In the midnight service especially, there was an expectant hush that went beyond the usual reverent silence before the service, and someone said that, for the first time in her life, she had felt the sweet savor of the Christ child in her heart. . . .

As [Father Tim] headed home with Dooley* at nearly one-thirty in the morning, he felt deeply grateful, but uncommonly fatigued.

Father Tim had never been able to decide when to open his gifts. He could hardly do it on Christmas Eve, when he arrived home past 1:00 A.M. after preaching two services. And on Christmas morning, conducting two masses kept him at Lord's Chapel until well past noon.

"I play it by ear," he once told Emma, who couldn't imagine not opening presents anytime she felt like it, starting on or before December 15.

At nearly two o'clock in the morning, they sat on the floor with hot chocolate and Winnie's doughnuts, and he gave Dooley his presents from Miss Sadie, Puny, Emma, and one from himself: a wool scarf from the Collar Button.

Miss Sadie had sent two pocket handkerchiefs, a pair of shoelaces, and a five-dollar bill wrapped in aluminum foil and tied with a red ribbon. Puny had given him a yellow windbreaker, and there were two dozen Reese's Cups from Emma.

Dooley sat mournfully in the midst of his gifts. "I wanted 'at ol' bicycle."

"The way your earnings are piling up, you'll have it before long. Now, I'd like to open your present to me."

"Wait 'til mornin'. You ain't goin' t' like it anyway."

"I'd appreciate making that decision myself."

"Wait 'til morning. I'm give out," Dooley said, irritably.

It was two-thirty when the pair trudged upstairs, well behind [the dog] Barnabas, who was already sprawled at the foot of the bed and snoring. . . .

At six-thirty, he and Barnabas woke Dooley.

"I don't want t' git up!" he wailed. "You done wore me out goin' t' church. I ain't never been t' s' much church in my life. I didn't know they was that much church in th' whole dern world."

"My friend, you will be pleased to know that Santa Claus visited this humble rectory last night and left something in the study for one Dooley Barlowe."

*Dooley is a young orphan boy staying with Father Tim.

"They ain't no Santy. I don't believe 'at old poop."

"Well, then, lie there and believe what you like. I'm going downstairs and have my famous Christmas morning casserole."

Barnabas leaped on Dooley's bed and began licking his ear.

" 'is ol' dog is th' hatefulest thing I ever seen!" Dooley moaned, turning his face to the wall. . . .

—◦—

[Father Tim] set two places at the counter and took the bubbling sausage casserole from the oven. There would be no diet this day. Then, he turned on the record player and heard the familiar, if scratchy, strains of the *Messiah*. Dooley appeared at the kitchen door, dressed in the burgundy robe.

"Sounds like a' army's moved in down here."

"My friend, you have hit the nail on the head. It is an army of the most glorious voices in recent history, singing one of the most majestic musical works ever written!"

Dooley rolled his eyes.

"I believe you've been asked to sit with Jena Ivey and your Sunday school friends this morning, . . . is that correct?"

"Yeah."

"Yes, sir."

No response.

Directly after Christmas, he would deal with this pigheaded behavior to the fullest.

"I ain't feelin' too good."

"Is that right? What's the trouble?"

"I puked up somethin' green."

"Really?"

"It had a lot of brown in it, too."

"The walk to church will revive you. You've been going pretty strong, keeping to a rector's schedule. Why don't you look in the study and find out what Barnabas is up to?"

He followed the boy into the study, to see what he'd been imagining for weeks: the look of joyful astonishment on Dooley Barlowe's face. . . .

—◦—

Dooley really hadn't seemed well, Father Tim concluded, as he walked home from church. He'd promised to stay right there on the study sofa, looking at his new bicycle and drinking 7-Up.

Though he'd received three invitations to Christmas dinner with parishioners, he wanted nothing more than to go home and crash. Later, if Dooley felt up to it, they'd take the new bike to the school yard and over to the Presbyterian parking lot.

There was only one problem with that plan. . . . Dooley Barlowe had run away.

Handel's Gift

EVELYN PRATT SECREST, *Georgia*

One night in 1741, a bent old man shuffled listlessly down a dark London street. George Frederick Handel was starting out on one of the aimless, despondent wanderings that had become a nightly ritual for him. His mind was a battleground between hope based on his past glories and despair based on the future.

For forty years Handel had written stately music for the aristocracy of England and Europe. Kings and queens had showered him with honors. Then his jealous rivals had planted rowdies in the audience who broke up each performance of his operas. Court society turned against him, and Handel was reduced to poverty. Then a cerebral hemorrhage paralyzed his right side. Handel had sought healing from natural hot baths in France. Against his doctor's orders, he stayed in the scalding waters nine hours at a time and slowly his strength returned, and he could walk and move his hand again.

So he wrote four more operas, and honors were once again heaped upon him. But then his staunch patroness, Queen Caroline, died. A frigid winter gripped England, and since there was no way to heat the theaters, engagements were canceled, and Handel sank deeper and deeper into debt.

On this particular night he was nearing only fifty-six but felt hopelessly old and tired. Returning to his shabby lodging, he saw a bulky package on the desk. Tearing off the wrapping, he read

Handel's Messiah *was always a part of our family tradition, and we especially enjoyed my Grandmother's retelling of how Handel came to write this oratorio. Recently I inherited her journals from the 1950s and was delighted to find the story written down as I heard it so long ago and now share with you.*—L. S. M.

"Libretto: A Sacred Oratorio," with a letter expressing the wish that he begin immediately on the oratorio. The writer had added these words of encouragement "The Lord gave the Word . . ."

Now Handel was not a pious man. Yes, he did help unfortunates even when he could ill afford to, but he had a violent temper. "Why didn't he give me an opera to write?" he wailed as he listlessly thumbed through the words to the oratorio.

Then this passage caught his eye, "He was despised and rejected of men. . . . He looked for someone to have pity on Him but there was no man; neither found He any to comfort him."

With a glowing sense of kinship Handel read on, "He trusted in God. . . . God did not leave His soul in hell. . . . He will give you rest."

These words began to come alive and glow with meaning: "Wonderful, Counselor, I know that my Redeemer liveth, and Hallelujah!" Handel could feel the old fire being rekindled in his mind as wondrous melodies tumbled one over another. Grabbing a pen he started to write, and with incredible swiftness the notes filled page after page.

The next morning his manservant found Handel bent over his desk, so he put the breakfast tray within easy reach and slipped out. When he returned at noon, the food had been untouched. The servant watched as his master took a piece of bread, crushed it and let it fall to the floor.

Handel was consumed with writing and then jumping up and running to the harpsichord. At times he would stride up and down the room flailing the air with his arms and singing at the top of his lungs, "Hallelujah! Hallelujah!" the tears running down his cheeks.

"I've never seen him act like this before," confided the servant to a friend. "He just stares at me and doesn't see me. He says the gates of heaven are opened wide for him and that God himself is there. . . . I'm afraid he's going mad!"

For twenty-four days Handel labored like a fiend with little rest or food. Then he fell on his bed exhausted, with his new score, *Messiah*, laying on his desk. He slept for sixteen hours as though in a coma and then awoke bellowing for a tremendous amount of food. He laughed heartily and joked with the doctor who had been summoned to check on him. "If you have come for a friendly visit, I will like it, but I won't have you poking at my carcass. There's nothing the matter with me."

A vast audience thronged to hear the very first performance of *Messiah*. The King and Queen attended and spontaneously stood in reverence when the "Hallelujah Chorus" began. That custom has continued to this day. George Frederick Handel was beset with difficulties, but he never again succumbed to despair. Age sapped his vitality, he went blind, but his undaunted spirit remained to the last. One evening in 1750 Handel was present at a performance of *Messiah*. At the beginning of "The Trumpet Shall Sound" he felt faint and nearly fell. Friends helped him home to bed where he expressed a desire to die on Good Friday, April 13—the anniversary of the first presentation of *Messiah*. And so his soul departed his worn body, but his spirit made glorious went home to glory.

Through his oratorio Handel lit a torch that has been carried around the world. Truly God's Word poured through his mind to his pen and into the music that healed his ailing body and soul. And now uncounted millions have joined in spirit to sing and be healed by the "Hallelujah Chorus."

The kingdom of this world has become
the Kingdom of the Lord and of His Christ,
and He shall reign forever and ever.
King of Kings and Lord of Lords. Hallelujah!
For the Lord God Omnipotent reigneth.
Hallelujah! Hallelujah! Hallelujah!

SECTION III

"It was again Christmas in the Old South."

Christmas Is Come

VIRGINIA ALMANACK, *Eighteenth century*

Christmas is come, hang on the pot,

Let spits turn round, and ovens be hot;

Beef, pork, and poulty, now provide

To feast thy neighbors at this tide.

Christmas in
the Old South

H E R B E R T   W E R N E C K E

Christmas on the plantation was not just a day for children—it was a season to be enjoyed by everyone. Preparations began right after Thanksgiving with the baking and storing away of the first Christmas cakes. From then on it was one grand and glorious round of "fixin'."

Except for a few of the "store-bought'n" gifts, the land itself provided all that was needed—the pigs for roasting, the hams, the turkeys, and all the delicious puddings and dressings, preserves, jellies, jams, pickles, peppers, sweet potatoes, nuts, and all the countless delights of southern cooking. The woods and fields provided the hickory logs and pine knots for the fireplace; the holly, mistletoe, and evergreen boughs for the decorations; the partridges and rabbits to round out the Christmas menus.

Everything was cleaned and polished to shining perfection, and when Christmas Eve arrived the plantation was rich with color and sound. When the old cowbell rang summoning everyone to the watch-night meeting in the Quarters, Christmas Eve had arrived. Solemn old hymns were sung until midnight, and prayers were offered by the earnest voices.

With the arrival of cock's crow announcing the holy hour, the prayers turned to rejoicing and dancing and singing—and it was Christmas! Then everyone rushed into the Big House with a shout of "Christmas Gift!" and with games, feasting, and song, the week-long festival was launched. It was again Christmas in the Old South.

How to Make a Great Cake

MARTHA CUSTIS, *Virginia 1781*

From an old manuscript dated "Mt. Vernon, 1781" and made by Martha Custis Washington for her grandmama.

Take forty eggs and divide the whites from the yolks, and beat them to a froth.

Then work four pounds of butter to a cream, and put the whites of the eggs to it, a tablespoonful at a time, until it is well worked.

Then put four pounds of sugar, finely powdered, to it in the same manner.

Then put in the yolks of eggs and five pounds of flour and five pounds of fruit.

Two hours will bake it.

Add to it one-half an ounce of mace, one nutmeg, one-half pint of wine and some French brandy.

Rise Up Shepherd and Follow

This African-American carol probably dates from the late eighteenth or early nineteenth century. The verses are usually sung by a solo voice, with a chorus echo of "Rise up, shepherd, and follow."

There's a star in the east on Christmas morn.
    Rise up, shepherd and follow.
It will lead to the place where the Savior's born.
    Rise up, shepherd and follow.
Leave your ewes and leave your lambs.
    Rise up, shepherd and follow.
Leave your sheep and leave your rams.
    Rise up, shepherd and follow.
Follow, follow. Rise up, shepherd and follow.
Follow the star of Bethlehem.
    Rise up, shepherd and follow.

If you take good heed to the angel's word,
    Rise up, shepherd and follow.
You'll forget your flock you'll forget your herd.
    Rise up, shepherd and follow.
Leave your ewes and leave your lambs.
    Rise up, shepherd and follow.
Leave your sheep and leave your rams.
    Rise up, shepherd and follow.
Follow, follow. Rise up, shepherd and follow.
Follow the star of Bethlehem.
    Rise up, shepherd and follow.

Silent Nights, Southern Nights

RANDALL BEDWELL, *Tennessee*

The South, it seems, celebrated Christmas before any other region of America. We know that the Spanish observed the holiday during their southern interlude, and so did the settlers in Jamestown, Virginia. In fact, the famous story about Pocahontas saving the life of Captain John Smith takes place at Christmastime (December 31, 1607, to be exact). In the 1830s, Arkansas, Louisiana, and Alabama became the first states in the nation to declare Christmas a legal holiday.

Due to the land-rich, agricultural economy that has defined the region since its settlement, Christmas in the antebellum South served as more a social than a religious occasion. Secular festivities filled the leisure time of all classes during the natural interruption of seasonal work cycles. Many southern holiday culinary traditions, such as goose, ham, turkey, mincemeat pies, and brandied peaches, originated from the dishes served at these early Yuletide galas. From beginning to end, residents of the Old South celebrated Christmas throughout several days, or even weeks, and it was never "over and done with" in a single day. During the Civil War, Christmas grew more popular in the North, while the holiday resourcefulness of Southerners was sorely tested.

By the turn of the century, with increasing urbanization and the rise of the "Bible Belt" during the New South era, southern Christmases had taken on more Christian, and commercial, overtones. Tennessee author Will Allen Dromgoole, the "Southern Dickens" in her lifetime, commingles the two themes in her 1895 short story "Christmas at the Corner Grocery." The tale concerns a poor store clerk. (Picture Bob Cratchet, with not one but two "tiny Tims," at work on Christmas Eve. His boss—a southern Scrooge in every way except for his own domestic holiday celebration—is at home living it up with his family.) Although he does not have the money to contribute to charity at Christmas, the kindhearted clerk gives all the customers—black and white—items they want (but cannot afford) from the store's stock. He then adds the cost to his own account in the company ledger, all the while watching his debt to his employer grow at an alarming rate. Later that night, the benevolent clerk has a dream in which he peeks into God's ledger—the "Book of Life" itself. There he beholds a balanced account, indicative of salvation, beside his own name.

By and large, southern Christmas traditions remain vital and intact heading into the twenty-first century. The South most definitely has influenced the nation's image of Christmas. Such contributions as the popular "country Christmas" decorating concept, Haddon Sundblom's famous "Coca-Cola Santa Claus," and numerous Christmas pop standards (including Gene Autry's "Rudolph the Red-Nosed Reindeer") demonstrate a deep and abiding belief in the unique power of Christmas and the special affinity of Southerners for the yuletide season.

A Gift on Christmas Eve

One Christmas Eve, Ira D. Sankey was traveling by steamboat up the Delaware River. Asked to sing, Mr. Sankey sang the "Shepherd Song," or "Savior Like a Shepherd Lead Us." After the song was ended, a man with a rough, weather-beaten face came up to Mr. Sankey and said: "Did you ever serve in the Union Army?"

"Yes," answered Mr. Sankey, "in the spring of 1860."

"Can you remember if you were doing picket duty on a bright, moonlit night in 1862?"

"Yes," answered Mr. Sankey, very much surprised.

"So did I," said the stranger, "but I was serving in the Confederate Army. When I saw you standing at your post, I said to myself: 'That fellow will never get away from here alive.' I raised my musket and took aim. I was standing in the shadow completely concealed, while the full light of the moon was falling upon you.

"At that instant, just as a moment ago, you raised your eyes to heaven and began to sing. Music, especially song, has always had a wonderful power over me, and I took my finger off the trigger. 'Let him sing his song to the end,' I said to myself. 'I can shoot him afterwards. He's my victim at all events, and my bullet cannot miss him.' But the song you sang then was the song you sang just now. I heard the words perfectly:

> We are Thine, do Thou befriend us,
> Be the guardian of our way.

"Those words stirred up many memories in my heart. I began to think of my childhood and my God-fearing mother. She had many, many times sung that song to me. But she died all too soon; otherwise much in my life would no doubt have been different.

"When you had finished your song it was impossible for me to take aim at you again. I thought: 'The Lord who is able to save that man from certain death must surely be great and mighty' and my arm of its own accord dropped limp at my side."

Ira Sankey, song leader for evangelist Dwight L. Moody, never forgot this encounter, which to him was a true gift of life one Christmas Eve.

Robert E. Lee Writes to His Wife

DECEMBER 25, 1861,
DURING THE CIVIL WAR

Dear Mary,

I cannot let this day of grateful rejoicing pass
without some communion with you. I am thankful
for the many among the past that I have passed
with you, and the remembrance of them fills me
with pleasure. As to our old home, if not
destroyed it will be difficult ever to be recognized.
. . . It is better to make up our minds to a general
loss. They cannot take away the remembrances of
the spot, and the memories of those that to us ren-
dered it sacred. That will remain to us as long as
life will last and that we can preserve.

Christmas of '62

WILLIAM G. MCCABE, *in the army of Northern Virginia, during the Civil War, 1862*

The wintry blast goes wailing by,
    The snow is falling overhead;
I hear the lonely sentry's tread,
    And distant watch-fires light the sky.

Dim forms go flitting through the gloom;
    The soldiers cluster round the blaze
To talk of other Christmas days,
    And softly speak of home and home.

My sabre swinging overhead,
    Gleams in the watch-fire's fitful glow,
While fiercely drives the blinding snow,
    And memory leads me to the dead.

My thoughts go wandering to and fro,
    Vibrating 'twixt the Now and Then;
I see the low-browed home agen,
    The old hall wreathed with mistletoe.

And sweetly from the far-off years
    Comes borne the laughter faint and low,
The voices of the Long Ago!
    My eyes are wet with tender tears.

I feel agen the mother kiss,
    I see agen the glad surprise
That lighted up the tranquil eyes
    And brimmed them o'er with tears of bliss,

As, rushing from the old hall-door,
    She fondly clasped her wayward boy—
Her face all radiant with the joy
    She felt to see him home once more.

My sabre swinging on the bough
    Gleams in the watch-fire's fitful glow,
While fiercely drives the blinding snow
    Aslant upon my saddened brow.

Those cherished faces are all gone!
    Asleep within the quiet graves
Where lies the snow in drifting waves—
    And I am sitting here alone.

There's not a comrade here to-night
    But knows that loved ones far away
On bended knees this night will pray:
    "God, bring our darling from the fight."

But there are none to wish me back,
    For me no yearning prayers arise.
The lips are mute and closed the eyes—
    My home is in the bivouac.

The Poinsettia

AN AMERICAN CHRISTMAS FLOWER

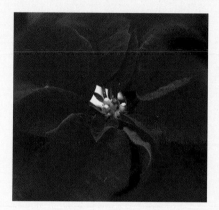

Most flowers, herbs, and plants used at Christmas are associated with very ancient celebrations. But the poinsettia is an addition of a much later date, the New World's contribution to Christmas. In 1825, Joel Roberts Poinsett of South Carolina, a diplomat who was the first American minister to Mexico, became intrigued with the brilliant red "flowers" topping spindly shrubs all over the countryside. The local people called them "flame flowers" or "flowers of the Holy Night" because they were used as decorations in Mexican Nativity processions.

In Mexican legend, a small boy knelt at the altar of his village church on Christmas Eve. He had nothing to offer the Christ child on his birthday because the boy had no money. But his prayers were sincere, and a miracle gave him the present that could be bought by no one: the first Flower of the Holy Night sprang up at his feet in brilliant red and green homage to the holy birth. Thus was born the flower we know as the Poinsettia.

Dr. Joel Roberts Poinsett was the American ambassador to Mexico from 1825 to 1829. His keen interest in botany made him very interested in the Flower of the Holy Night, and he brought it back to his home in South Carolina. It became very popular as a Christmas plant and was named after him.

SECTION IV

Traditions and Hospitality

"Christmas was really just a time for
everybody getting together."

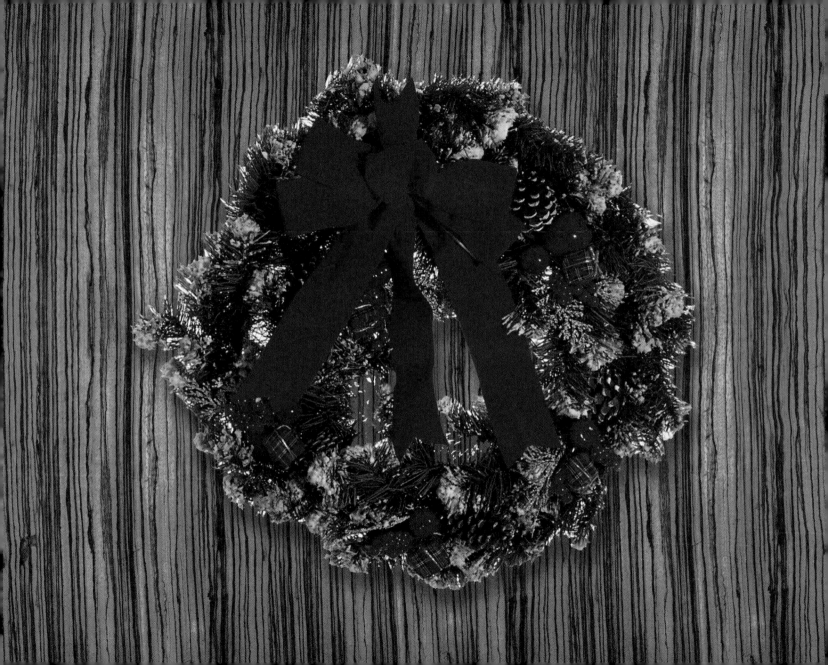

We Used That Star for Years

MARGARET BULGIN, *North Carolina*

One thing that contributed to our Christmas [during the Depression years] was the fact that my mother had a sister who never married. She took it as her Christian duty to provide packages at Christmas for all her nieces and nephews. The first yo-yo I ever saw came in a package from Aunt Louise at Christmas. She always included clothes, dresses, scarves, gloves, and things like that, but there'd be some foolishness, too. And always peanut brittle. She always sent peanut brittle. But not everybody had an Aunt Louise, and we knew we were very fortunate to have her.

When I was eleven or twelve years old, I wanted a suitcase worse than anything in the world. I had no intention of ever going anywhere. I didn't have any notion of traveling, but I wanted a suitcase, and I got one for Christmas that year. It was a nice little suitcase—black cardboard and a green lining—looked like taffeta. I bet that thing cost at least three or four dollars! That was what I wanted, and it was there! I just loved it! I put it up in my closet, and I guess I eventually used it.

'Course we didn't have any electric lights, so our Christmas trees didn't look like they do now. We were never allowed to use candles. They're just so tricky. And Father, being in the fire-fighting business, wasn't about to let us do that anyway. We made a lot of our ornaments at home out of craft paper—mostly paper chains. Mother would bake gingerbread men. I remember very well a little sheep, a cookie cutout, that she made of gingerbread. We hung those on the tree. We made everything except for a few store-bought ornaments that Aunt Louise sent us. At school, we'd also make a star to go on top of the tree there. Before the Christmas holidays, we always did these things in school and brought them home. I can remember when the first tin foil came out. We cut a star out of cardboard and covered it in tin foil. That shiny star was the first one I remember. We used that star for years.

We'd kill a hog usually between Thanksgiving and Christmas—after the weather got cold and the meat wouldn't be as likely to spoil. They would save the bladders out of the hogs and blow them up like balloons and let them dry. They'd make an explosion when we jumped on them and popped them. We'd usually do that on Christmas Eve. It would be louder than the burst of a balloon. Made a noise kind of like a gunshot.

When I was growing up, we almost always had Christmas dinner at my grandmother's. She lived within walking distance from our house. Mother would cook the pork roast and bring it and all the baking she'd done, and we'd go to Grandmother's. One of my aunts lived up the road with her big family, and they would come down to Grandmother's, so it was bedlam there! Just a big family. Christmas was really just a time for everybody getting together.

Miss Daisy's Party Sausage Balls

DAISY KING, *Tennessee*

Gourmet cooks may cringe at this recipe, but everyone knows that it is a must have for any true southern holiday gathering. Serve with bright-colored toothpicks. L. S. M.

3 cups Bisquick or biscuit mix

1 pound hot sausage

1 10-ounce package cheddar cheese, grated

2 tablespoons dried parsley flakes

1 tablespoon Worcestershire sauce

1 teaspoon minced onion

1 teaspoon black pepper

1 teaspoon oregano

1 teaspoon garlic powder

Assemble all ingredients and utensils. In a bowl, combine all ingredients and mix well. Roll into small balls. Place on ungreased baking sheet and bake in oven at 375 degrees for 15 to 20 minutes or until brown. Serve warm. Yield: about 100 sausage balls.

Holiday Eggnog

This is most definitely not Mamalu's recipe, but an alternative for those who prefer a nonalcoholic version of this traditional favorite. L. S. M.

4 eggs, separated

1/2 cup sugar

2 cups cold milk

1 cup cold light cream

1 1/2 teaspoons vanilla

1/8 teaspoon salt

1/4 teaspoon nutmeg

Beat egg yolks and 1/4 cup sugar until thick and cream colored; gradually add milk, cream, vanilla, salt, and 1/8 teaspoon nutmeg and beat until frothy. Beat egg whites with remaining sugar until soft peaks form, and fold in. Cover and chill until serving time. Mix well, pour into punch bowl, and sprinkle with remaining nutmeg. About 250 calories per serving. Makes 6 servings.

Creating Christmas Memories

LUCINDA SECREST MCDOWELL, *Georgia*

On the first Sunday of Advent, we put up our Christmas tree. Each of our four children has a box of carefully wrapped ornaments with his or her name on it. What fun it is to examine them each year and remember other Christmases in other locations! None of the ornaments are particularly fancy or expensive. But each one is special. This is why. . . .

When I was a little girl growing up in Georgia, my Mama gave me and my two sisters a new ornament each Christmas. She carefully inscribed our name and the year. "This is so when you grow up and have a tree of your own, you'll already have lots of familiar decorations," she lovingly explained.

When I got my first apartment after college graduation, I had twenty ornaments to put on my small tree. By the time I got married, I had thirty-one—each inscribed with my name and the date. Remembering the sense of family and continuity it brought me in my early adult years, I decided to do the same thing for my children.

Each November I purchase or make four ornaments symbolic of something that happened that year, and I write in a gold pen the names of Justin, Timothy, Fiona, and Margaret. These are put at their places on our Thanksgiving Day table, just in time for tree decorating.

No, our tree will never win any awards or be found on the pages of *House Beautiful*. The decorations on it are not color-coordinated nor of any particular theme, which seems so popular these days. But our tree reflects our family—the ups and downs, the victories and defeats. And we bring them all to the manger each year, celebrating with joy the birth of our Savior, Jesus Christ!

Not Celebrate?

ANN WEEMS, *Tennessee*

Not celebrate?

Your burden is too great to bear?

Your loneliness is intensified during this Christmas season?

Your tears seem to have no end?

Not celebrate?

You should lead the celebration!

You should run through the streets

    to ring the bells and sing the loudest!

You should fling the tinsel on the tree,

    and open your house to your neighbors,

    and call them in to dance!

It is unto you that a Savior is born this day,

    One who comes to lift your burden from your shoulders,

    One who comes to wipe the tears from your eyes.

You are not alone,

    for he is born this day to you.

Tennessee Ernie Ford's Cornbread and Sausage Holiday Dressing

TENNESSEE ERNIE FORD

This is good for making two pans—you might want to double up if you've got a big crew comin' over! First off, here's what you'll need:

Enough cornmeal mix to make
two good-sized pans of corn bread
(Yellow or white . . . it's up to you.)

One or two packages of turkey giblets
*(Make sure you've got it all—
neck, gizzards, liver, and heart.)*

Two pounds of hot and spicy pork sausage
(Don't get the mild . . . you'll take the tang out of it!)

One bunch each of celery and green onions

One bay leaf

Powdered sage

Black pepper

Now, here's what you do:

DAY ONE

After you've finished breakfast, pull out a big, deep stew pot and pour just a little water in the bottom.

Unwrap your giblet packages, rinse the giblets off, and place them in the pot. (Don't cut anything up—that comes later.) Add more water until the giblets are covered.

Get that bay leaf out and toss it in there.

Measure out close to 1/2 teaspoon of sage, rub it between your hands (did you wash?), and dust it into your pot. Add two healthy pinches of black pepper.

Cover the pot, and put it on the back burner, somewhere between simmer and low—no higher!—we're going to let things steep just about all day.

Check the water level every once in a while, making sure the giblets stay covered.

After supper, take the pot off the stove and set it to one side, letting it cool a little on its own. Then, just before you hit the sack, put it in the fridge for the night. (Keep the lid on!)

DAY TWO

(Doesn't your kitchen smell great this morning?!) In a couple of standard 1-inch deep baking pans, bake your two pones of cornbread. While they're baking, take your pot of giblets and broth out of the fridge, and warm things up just a tad.

Get your best iron skillet out, unwrap your sausage, pinch it off in chunks, and brown all two pounds of it. Drain the grease off, and set the sausage to one side.

Take your celery and onions out and chop them real fine.

Take that pot of giblets off the stove, and . . . whoa! get that cornbread out of the oven!

While your cornbread's cooling, take all the giblets out of the pot, get that bay leaf out of there, and set the broth to one side.

Cut, slice, chop, and pull all your giblet meat up (it'll peel right off that neck bone. . . .).

Get out the two BIGGEST mixing bowls you've got. Crumble both your pones of cornbread up into both bowls.

Add your browned sausage, your giblet meat, and your chopped greens to your cornmeal. (Make sure you've got a good, balanced mix in each mixing bowl.)

Now, slowly add your broth to each mixture, one bowl at a time. Get your hands in there (did you wash?), and go for it until you've got a nice, consistent, moist mix. Moisture is the key word . . . you don't want your dressing to be dry.

Get your baking pans back out and level off each pan with your dressing mix. If you've got any broth left over, lightly pour the remainder over the top of each pan of dressing.

Put both pans in the oven at around 350–375 degrees for about 20 minutes, or until you've got a nice, light brown, moist sheen on top.

Are you ready? Call everybody to dinner. Say Grace, and watch your dressing disappear.

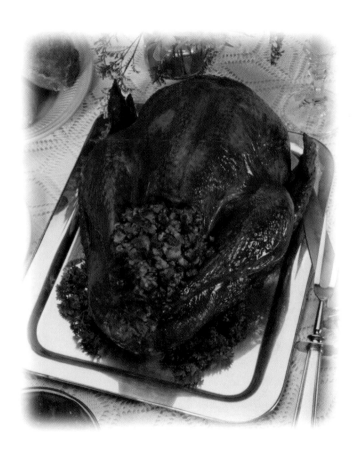

Overnight Turkey

LUCINDA SECREST MCDOWELL, *Georgia*

I have cooked all my turkeys this way for the past seventeen years, and each time folks comment on how tasty they are. It also leaves me free to enjoy the holiday because the turkey is already done! L. S. M.

About an hour before you go to bed, preheat oven to 500 degrees.

Wash turkey and empty cavity of giblets (do not stuff turkey).

Rub outside of turkey with olive oil.

Put turkey in roaster and pour 5 cups of water over it. Place a tight-fitting lid on roaster and bake at 500 degrees for one hour. DO NOT TAKE OFF LID AT ANY TIME.

After one hour, turn down oven to very lowest level (without actually turning it off). Leave turkey in oven and go to bed! Wake up to a bird that is tender, juicy, brown, and ready. Spend the rest of your morning cooking other things. This really works!

Flora Mae's Biscuits

FLORA MAE HUNTER, *Georgia*

3 cups flour

3/4 cup Crisco shortening

3/4 cup sweet milk

1/2 teaspoon salt

2 teaspoons baking powder

Mix 2 heaping teaspoons baking powder, flour, Crisco, and salt. Keep mixing the flour until smooth. Do not mix all the flour. Add milk slowly. Add remaining flour; do not over-work the dough. Put on a floured board and roll out about 3/4 of an inch. Cut with a biscuit cutter, making about 15 biscuits. Bake in a 400-degree oven until brown, bottom and top. If you have flour left over, resift and save.

When someone asked a friend, after his first stay in the South, what impressed him most, he promptly replied, "The invariable advice given by every hostess as the biscuits were passed: 'Take two, and butter them while they're hot.'"

Another visitor from the North tells this story. Returning home after a sojourn in Dixie, someone asked him how he liked the southern biscuits.

"Never tasted one," he replied.

"Never tasted a *biscuit?*" echoed the friend. "Why, I've been told they have them for every meal."

"And so they do," said the weary traveler, "for breakfast, dinner, and supper, but I was never allowed to eat one. Every time they were passed I would take one and butter it according to directions. And, invariably, just as I would get it to my mouth, my arm would be seized and someone would cry, 'Don't eat that. It's cold. The hot ones are just coming in.' So, I would relinquish my morsel, take another, butter it and put it down, and before I could eat it, the hot ones would appear, and the whole thing began over again."

Hattie Mae's Cornbread

HATTIE MAE JONES, *Georgia*

This is my favorite cornbread but of course, like all the best cooks, Hattie rarely consulted a recipe. But since she had to write it down for me, I'm glad to share it. L. S. M.

2 cups cornmeal

1 1/2 cups milk

2 tablespoons shortening

2 tablespoons baking powder

1 teaspoon salt

1 tablespoon sugar

Mix all together and put in greased square pan or loaf pan. Bake at 450 degrees in hot oven about a half-hour or until brown.

Sweet Potato Pie

LUCINDA SECREST MCDOWELL, *Georgia*

1 9-inch deep dish pie shell, prebaked

1/4 cup butter or margarine, softened

3 eggs, beaten

1 teaspoon vanilla

a pinch of salt

1/4 teaspoon nutmeg

1/4 cup brown sugar

2 1/4 cups mashed sweet potatoes that have
been baked or boiled, then peeled

2/3 cup sugar

1/4 cup milk

1 cup nuts, chopped
(I use pecans.)

In large mixing bowl, cream together softened butter with sugar. Add beaten eggs, milk, vanilla, nutmeg, and salt. With mixer at low speed, add mashed sweet potatoes. Mix until all ingredients are blended and the mixture is smooth.

Pour into prebaked pie shell. Bake in preheated 350-degree oven for 30 minutes. After removing from oven, sprinkle chopped nuts and brown sugar on top of the pie. Then bake 15 minutes longer. Let pie cool and top with marshmallows if desired. Makes 6–8 servings.

SECTION V

"It was my most memorable Christmas."

My Most Memorable Christmas

CATHERINE MARSHALL, *Virginia*

Why is one Christmas more memorable than another?

It seldom has anything to do with material gifts. In fact, poor circumstances often bring out the creativity in a family.

But I think the most memorable Christmases are tied in somehow with family milestones: reunions, separations, births and, yes, even death. Perhaps that is why Christmas, 1960, stands out so vividly in my memory.

We spent that Christmas at Evergreen Farm in Lincoln, Virginia—the home of my parents. With us were my sister and her husband—Emmy and Harlow Hoskins—and their two girls, Lynn and Winifred. It meant a typical family occasion with our three children, Linda, Chester and Jeffrey, along with Peter John who was then a senior at Yale. Five children can make an old farmhouse ring with the yuletide spirit.

For our Christmas Eve service, Lynn and Linda had prepared an improvised altar before the living room fireplace. Jeffrey and Winifred (the youngest grandchildren) lighted all the candles. Then with all of his family gathered around him, my father read Luke's incomparable account of the first Christmas. There was carol singing, with Chester and Winifred singing a duet, "Hark, the Herald Angels Sing," in their high piping voices. Then my mother, the story-teller of the family, gave us an old favorite, "Why the Chimes Rang." She made us see the ragged little boy creeping up that long cathedral aisle and slipping his gift onto the altar.

Then she said, "You know, I'd like to make a suggestion to the family. The floor underneath the tree in the den is piled high with gifts we're giving to one another. But we're celebrating Christ's birthday not each other's. This is His time of year. What are we going to give to Jesus?"

The room began to hum with voices, comparing notes. But Mother went on, "Let's think about it for a few moments. Then we'll go around the circle and each of us will tell what gift he will lay on the altar for Christ's birthday."

Chester, age seven, crept close to his father for a whispered consultation. Then he said shyly, "What I'd like to give Jesus this year is not to lose my temper anymore."

Jeffrey, age four, who had been slow in night training, was delightfully specific, "I'll give Him my diapers."

Winifred said softly that she was going to give Jesus good grades in school. Len's was, "To be a better father, which means a gift of more patience."

And so it went . . . on around the group. Peter John's

was short but significant. "What I want to give to Christ is a more dedicated life." I was to remember that statement five years later at the moment of his ordination into the Presbyterian ministry when he stood so straight and so tall and answered so resoundingly, "I do so believe. . . . I do so promise. . . ." Yes at Christmastime, 1960, the ministry was probably the last thing he expected to get into.

Then it was my father's turn. "I certainly don't want to inject too solemn a note into this," he said, "but somehow I know that this is the last Christmas I'll be sitting in this room with my family gathered around me like this."

We gasped and protested, but he would not be stopped. "No, I so much want to say this. I've had a most wonderful life. Long, long ago I gave my life to Christ. Though I've tried to serve Him, I've failed Him often. But He has blessed me with great riches—especially my family. I want to say this while you're all here. I may not have another chance. Even after I go on into the next life, I'll still be with you. And, of course, I'll be waiting for each one of you there."

There was love in his brown eyes—and tears in ours. No one said anything for a moment. Time seemed to stand still in the quiet room. Firelight and candlelight played on the children's faces as they looked at their grandfather, trying to grasp what he was saying. The fragrance of balsam and cedar was in the air. The old windowpanes reflected back the red glow of Christmas lights.

Father did leave this world four months later—on May 1st. His passing was like a benediction. It happened one afternoon as he sat quietly in a chair in the little village post office talking to some of his friends. His heart just stopped beating. That Christmas Eve he had known with a strange sureness that the time was close.

Every time I think of Father now, I can see that scene in the living room—like a jewel of a moment set in the ordinary moments that make up our days. For that brief time real values came clearly into focus: Father's gratitude for life; Mother's strong faith; my husband's quiet strength; my son's inner yearning momentarily shining through blurred youthful ambitions; the eager faces of children groping toward understanding and truth; the reality of the love of God as our thoughts focused on Him whose birth we were commemorating.

It was my most memorable Christmas.

The Leftover Doll

LUCINDA SECREST MCDOWELL, *Georgia*

What do you mean you don't want a doll for Christmas?" Mama asked. "You've been talking of nothing else for months, Cindy!"

"Well . . . I don't," I stated. "Everybody gets a doll for Christmas, and I don't want to be like everybody else!"

Mama looked at me standing there with arms crossed and chest out. She lowered her voice to a gentle pleading, "Cindy, are you *sure?*"

"I am, Mama, really I am. I'm seven years old and I really don't need a doll," I said, trying to sound grown up.

Weeks passed with the usual holiday hubbub of pageants, parties, and present-wrapping. Finally, the long-awaited moment arrived—Christmas morning!

My sisters and I knew we had to stay at the top of the staircase until Mama and Daddy came to get us, so we got as close as we could and peered into the shadows of the living room at the mysterious bundles that flanked the central fireplace.

Santa left our gifts in the same place each year: Cathy's to the left of the fireplace in the big wing chair, Susan's to the right of the fireplace in the love seat, and mine (because I was, after all, the middle child) right in the middle—front and center!

"Merry Christmas! Everybody up!" boomed my daddy's laughing voice. No matter that we'd been up for hours. Whenever he awakened, the word was, "Everybody up!"

"Hmmmm . . . looks like Santa must have been here—all he left are cookie crumbs and an empty milk glass," Daddy said with a chuckle.

"Surely that isn't *all* he's left, Daddy?" four-year-old Susan softly inquired, her big blue eyes wide. She not only looked like an angel, she acted like one.

"Don't be silly!" Cathy said, worldly wise at age ten. She had Santa pretty well figured out. "Oooh, I can't believe it! He brought me a Poor Pitiful Pearl doll!"

I stopped to gaze at what was perhaps the ugliest doll I had ever seen. Fortunately, Poor Pitiful Pearl was a somewhat short-lived success, designed to play on the pity and compassion of young girls. Nonetheless, Cathy had wanted her and Cathy had gotten her.

"Mama, look—it's Thumbelina!" was all Susan could say as she cradled the soft baby doll in her arms, cooing and clucking just as Mama had done to her not so long ago. Thumbelina Secrest was clearly the new baby of our family.

I focused on my own pile of gifts. To this day, I don't remember what Santa brought. My only memories are of what was so obviously missing—a doll.

My secret disappointment did not spoil Christmas Day nor our family gathering. I always looked forward to the annual tape-recording session with Daddy when he interviewed us and we got to perform whatever songs or poetry or Bible verses we had learned that year. Perry Como, Frank Sinatra, and Judy Garland serenaded us with Christmas favorites on the hi-fi, and all was cozy.

I was almost too sleepy to talk with my friend, Cax, when she called, reminding me of our new tradition of sharing the day after Christmas together.

"Oh, and don't forget to bring your new doll," Cax said, and hung up before I could tell her I didn't have a new doll.

The next day Mama helped me pack my overnight things. "Cindy, was it kind of hard not getting a doll when your sisters both got one?" she asked.

"Not at all!" I said, a bit too cheerily. "I had a great Christmas, Mama."

But this wise woman, all of thirty-three, could read me like a book. I've always worn my heart on my sleeve, and on the way to Cax's house, it broke open.

"Mama!" I cried, "I *did* want a doll, but I just didn't *know* I wanted one, so I told you I *didn't* want one, but I knew you would know that I really *did*, but instead you believed me, and so I *didn't* get a doll, but now I *want* one and I'm going to Cax's to play dolls, but I don't *have* one, and I know this makes me seem ungrateful 'cause I had such a nice Christmas, but Mama . . ."

"Yes, Cindy?"

"I really *did* want a doll."

"I see," she said.

I know now that even though she was frustrated, her heart was probably breaking and she was praying like crazy for God's guidance. I know that now, because I, too, have a seven-year-old daughter who is named for my mother, but who acts just like me.

"Cindy?"

"Yes, Mama?"

"How many times have I *told* you that actions have consequences? If you go around declaring to the world that you don't want a doll for Christmas, then you shouldn't be surprised when you don't get one!"

"Yes, Ma'am."

Mama's "actions-have-consequences" sermon had hit home. But today I learned that my mother longed to give me good gifts. She looked at me and smiled.

"Cindygirl, let's go find a doll!"

Now, back in the sixties, small-town Georgia didn't have such things as giant toy stores or discount marts. We were your basic two-block downtown with small department stores at either end and one in the middle. And the stock of dolls was usually depleted long before Christmas. Our chances of finding a doll were slim, but our hearts were high as we trudged from one store to another. After striking out twice, we were met at the final counter by a sympathetic clerk who peered down at me.

"Why, yes, honey, I do have one doll left, but I don't think you'll want her. Still . . . it's a shame nobody took her home for Christmas."

She walked into the back room and returned with a hard plastic doll with curly red hair and brown eyes. I could easily see why this doll had been passed over for the more popular soft-skinned, blond, blue-eyed babies. But what a *perfect* doll for someone like me who always liked to be just a little different!

Mama's eyes met mine. She instinctively knew that this doll was the one that would bring me true Christmas joy, all the more precious because I didn't deserve her.

"Mama, I love her already. Thank you so much— you're the bestest mama in the whole wide world!" I gushed, as we walked to the station wagon. "But what shall I name her?"

Without skipping a beat, Mama replied, "Joy. Why don't you call her *Joy?*"

It was a prophetic name. From that first sleepover at Cax's, Joy Secrest accompanied me everywhere. I kept a baby book documenting her family tree, first words, favorite foods, and birthday, December 26, 1960. She even wore my hand-me-down baby clothes. And she appears in almost all of my childhood photographs.

Forty years later, Joy and all her belongings are comfortably ensconced in my memory trunk down in our basement. She survived my childhood, but suffered a few breaks during xvisits with my own children.

Joy was always more than a doll to me. She was a symbol of my mother's love—a love that understood my childish immaturity and extended grace to me.

The Reason for the Season

LIZ CURTIS HIGGS, *Kentucky*

There were years when I didn't even have a Christmas tree, those single adult years through my twenties and early thirties when money was tight and a tree-for-one didn't sound like much fun. Usually, I worked Christmas day. Radio stations are an every-day-of-the-year kind of business, so rather than let my married friends work and miss time with their families, I always volunteered to do the morning show on Christmas. (Don't be impressed . . . I also got paid double time!)

It was December 25, 1984, and there I was on Christmas morning, standing in the studio, the only person in the building other than a security guard and a news reporter. I was feeling very sorry for myself—all alone, no phone callers, no visitors, just me—spinning carols and hymns on the turntables while big tears ran down my cheeks.

"Nobody loves me, Lord!" I said aloud in my most forlorn voice. "Nobody loves me!" I was sobbing by this point, feeling the most alone I'd ever felt in all my life. Then I heard his voice speaking to my heart as dearly and distinctly as the words on this page: "I love you, Liz. I love you."

My response was immediate and instinctive; I dropped to my knees. What love is this, that he would speak to me, his child, on Christmas morning! At that moment, the words of the music blasting out of the studio speakers penetrated my heart: "Joy to the world! The Lord is come!"

He came to us then, he comes to us now, and his message is still the same: "Have no fear of the cold. I love you!"

Appalachian Christmas

LYNDALL TOOTHMAN, *West Virginia*

When I was very small, we lived in a little log house back in the mountains of West Virginia. My sister was six years older than I was, and while I was growing up, it was just her and me until I was fifteen years old. Then, when my mother was forty-five, my brother was born. But until then, I was the boy of the family. I wore blue jeans from the time I can remember. Dad took me everywhere with him. I drove the horses and milked the cows and did everything that a boy would do. Dad would take me out in the hay field, and he and I would get the hay up and in better shape than our neighbor who had two boys, both of them older than I was. I was awful handy.

Now whenever Christmas came around, some of the neighbors decorated their homes, but we didn't until I was nearly grown. Then I went out and got a tree; but in my early childhood, I don't remember decorating at all.

We always decorated the church, though. We had a *big* Christmas tree there—usually a hemlock or a spruce—and everybody got together and we strung miles and miles of popcorn. If the weather was good, we would pick little red mountain tea berries and string them. And then we made the paper trimmings, these little colored paper chains.

My mother was quite handy with paper, and she made beautiful roses—you almost thought they were real. And they'd put mountain laurel and rhododendron around in the church. Then they'd have a Christmas program, and that was always a big thing. I remember that we were always in the Christmas program. I would usually have a little poem to say or something like that. And they always had the nativity scene and the shepherds and the angels and the cradle and the baby Jesus, and once in a while we'd have a live animal or two like a little donkey or a lamb.

We didn't have too much to go on, but we always had plenty to eat. My mother was an excellent cook, and I've seen her make dinner out of what anyone else would think was nothing at all—and make a good dinner. Now on Christmas Day, we didn't have the traditional Christmas dinner that the neighbors did. We had a special dinner that all of us looked forward to all year. And sometimes we would have to begin preparing for it three months before. The dinner consisted of fried country ham—we always cured our own meat—and red-eye gravy. I guess you all know what country ham and red-eye gravy is.

Then we had baked Irish potatoes and baked sweet potatoes, a pot of leather breeches beans, potato salad, dandelion salad, deviled eggs, hot raised biscuits, corn pone, jellies, jams, and preserves, three or four different kinds of homemade pickles, and we always had plenty of milk and butter. We also had either strawberry or dandelion wine. Then for dessert it was always boiled custard and Lady Baltimore white cake, and the children also had chestnuts. Some of our food was fairly unusual, which even our neighbors didn't do. But we thought they were great things.

Christmas Country

ANNE RIVERS SIDDONS, *Georgia*

It is perhaps a childish and wistful conceit, but the special country of Christmas is vivid and palpable to me. It is a place, a destination. You work through summer, through autumn, through the sorrowing waste of November. And there it is. It has been so, for me, since I was very small, and I think it will always be so.

What one sees from the threshold of Christmas is his alone, his own inner landscape. My Christmas country is forever that of a small southern town in the soft, wet, gray days of December, when streetlights wear opal collars. The time is always first dusk, when the lopsided evergreen trees in front of the freight depot bloom into primary colors, the wounded gaps where the power lines go through obscured in radiant clouds of Christmas light. Stores stay open late. The drugstore smells of Evening in Paris gift sets and cardboard-stale chocolate-covered cherries, and the dime store is glorious with fine gadgets and accordion-folded red paper bells, which will blossom out like Christmas roses.

White frame houses have pyramid-shaped electric candles in their windows, in front of the Venetian blinds, and their doors are dressed in foil, pine boughs, flat candy canes of red and white oilcloth. They are in full-dress regalia for the Garden Club decorating contest. One affluent door, more sophisticated than its fellows, wears a paper Santa Claus bought in Atlanta, and it never wins the prize.

Inside, in living rooms warm from coal fires in iron grates, Christmas trees are mostly pine, cut from somebody's woods or calf pasture and brought home behind a Ford tractor. The lights on them don't wink or bubble or twinkle. They go out frequently, with sullen abruptness, darkening one side of the tree and precipitating a scrambling search in the nest of extension cords buried in tissue paper underneath. But they give a sweet and sturdy light, and their heat on the drying needles produces a wonderful smell. That smell, and the exotic musk of cold oranges in Christmas morning stockings, is the official smell of Christmas to me still.

There is a manger scene on the brown lawn of the Methodist church, with a manger of rough-sawn planks made by the Men's League, a heavy cardboard Joseph and Mary, real straw, and an electric light bulb secreted in the straw to indicate the luminous presence of the Child. It is put up three weeks ahead of Christmas, our town's official announcement that the Day will come again this year.

Further on in Christmas country, there will be the traditional Methodist church Christmas tree, and a giant cedar will be donated and decorated and propped in secular glory at the red velvet altar cushion. Everyone will draw names and on the night of the Tree, the sanctuary will peal with oohs and ohs and you-*shouldn't*-haves, and the giddy giggling of children. Everyone gets a gift. When I was very small, about three, my father was superintendent of the Sunday School, and made an announcement early in December that the tree festivities would be held on such-and-such a date. I am told I escaped the clutches of my stricken mother, lurched down the aisle to where he stood, shrieked, "Preach some more about the Christmas tree, Daddy," had a truly heroic tantrum when he tried to quiet me, and was taken out in howling disgrace. A lot of my parents' friends still remember it.

About the time of the church Christmas tree, there will be a pageant, and the young of the church will be dressed in assorted biblical raiment and drilled and rehearsed and, finally, driven stiff-legged and numbed with terror out into the choir loft to reenact the Nativity. Throughout all the Christmases—for they roll into one and become instead of times, mileposts in Christmas country—I had some part in the pageant. Once, an angel, in a sheet, flapping great bumbling wings made of more sheet stretched over fencing wire and festooned with silver tinsel. Once, owing to a dearth of willing young men, a shepherd, in my father's maroon flannel bathrobe, with a turban made from a scarf. Once, in my early teens, a sullen and mortified Mary with a pillow under my choir robe. The reluctant Joseph to my Mary was a senior in high school and president of the Methodist Youth Fellowship, and I had a hopeless, aching, silent crush on him. I shall never forgive the pageant director, who said loudly just before we made our entrance, "For goodness' sake, Hal, hold her arm. And slow it down, Anne. You're *pregnant*."

On Christmas Eve, there are carols sung on front lawns courtesy of the MYF—galoshed and muffled against the raw silver fog that always shrouds this Christmas country—and people with sweaters thrown around their shoulders stand shivering on front porches and applaud the bleating "Si-i-lent Night! Ho-o-ly Night!" Somehow the night is, for a while, silent and holy.

Sometimes Coca-Cola is proffered to the carolers, and rich, heavy fruitcake made the year before in enamel pans and soaked all year with homemade wine under white muslin. On every hearth, another bottle of Coca-Cola and another slab of winy fruitcake waits for Santa Claus—surely a tipsy, reeking Santa when he finishes his rounds in our town. Cake and cola are always polished off by resigned parents.

On Christmas Eve, sleep is an unimaginable agony. I remember tossing mutely for what seemed black eternities, listening for the rattle of the lock at our front door that meant Santa Claus was coming in. I accepted the fact that he had to use the door because our chimneys were too small as unquestioningly as I accepted the profusion of Salvation Army Santas on every Atlanta street corner. I even bought it when I was told that in Fairburn he came in a truck, the climate being unsuitable for delicate reindeer hoofs. I don't remember the why of that. Otis Fletcher told me there was no Santa Claus when we were in the third grade; I must have been nearly eleven when I concluded that Otis hadn't been lying after all.

You do sleep, of course, though you will swear afterward you never closed your eyes. I took a solemn oath one Christmas, to my parents, that I had not only heard Santa Claus come in, but had seen him, and moreover, that Jack Benny and Mary Livingstone were with him. Whether to nip a budding liar in the bud or shatter one of childhood's most precious myths must have been a real dilemma for my parents. They solved it by admitting that perhaps I *had* seen Santa Claus, but I must have dreamed Jack Benny and Mary Livingstone, as they lived in Hollywood, California, and couldn't possibly have made it to Fairburn, Georgia, and back in time for their own Christmas morning.

You wake at four, and creep into your parents' room. "Is it time?" "No. Go back to bed."

And at five. And at five-thirty. At six, finally: "All right. It's time." Throughout my Christmas country, kids skin into bathrobes and slippers with bunny ears and race for the living room at six o'clock in the morning.

It is radiant and strange in the black pre-dawn. The tree is aflame. There is a coal fire burning. The Coca-Cola and fruitcake are gone; not a crumb remains. There are the presents brought by Santa Claus, piled unwrapped before the tree. The ones from parents and relatives have been wrapped and under the tree for two weeks, shaken into near-oblivion.

Somehow, the presents all seemed to be the same present, though, of course, they varied. From Santa Claus, a doll every year. One year she cried, another year she drank from a bottle and wet, one year she had "magic baby skin," one year she was an eternal bride-to-be, as frozen on the eve of her wedding as Keats's unravished bride of quietness. One year, when I was twelve, she was a truly exquisite Alice in Wonderland, a perfect, fragile mini-woman. Later that day, goaded by God knows what mute rebellion, spoiled perversity, what rampaging new hormones, I shot her with a new Daisy Air Rifle. My mother cried, and I cried and my father confiscated the air rifle. Dolls were gone from my Christmas country after that to be replaced by charm bracelets and pink angora sweaters and record albums, by the flimsy, useless, spangled Christmas things that I still love to receive.

There would be outfits. A nurse's outfit. A cowgirl outfit complete with fringed vest six-shooter and miniature western boots. An appalling WAC outfit, for we seemed perpetually at war in that holiday country. Somewhere in my parents' house, small, grave me sights along the six-shooter into the camera still; lumpy, unlovely me salutes an unknown Commander-in-Chief under the patent-leather bin of a hideous, flat-topped cap.

For my mother, a huge jar of blindingly purple bath salts that stank for days when she opened it. I had had my eye on it at Vickers's Five-and-Ten for half a year, and Mrs. Vickers had had to scrape the grime of unwantedness out of its mock cut-crystal when I purchased it. My father would open the miniature hatbox with the wonderful perfect little hat in it and a certificate that said he could receive the hat of his choice at an Atlanta hattery. Always, he said it was just exactly what he needed. Always, he bought the same hat.

Then Nellie would come from her small house directly behind ours, through the shrubbery hedge, to receive her ritual black rayon dress and help my mother begin our marathon Christmas dinner, and the current white spitz dog, one of an endless procession emanating from my grandfather's farm, would get his wrapped can of horsemeat, and I would be sent to dress in the burgundy velvet dress with the handmade white lace collar my grandmother made me every year. Relatives were coming.

Christmas dinner is always at noon in that country, and there are aunts and uncles, cousins who will break your toys by mid-afternoon, grandparents in unaccustomed ties and socks with clocks on them, and cameo brooches. Not all can come because of gas rationing, but an uncle who has a C card will collect those on his route, and they will arrive about eleven in the morning, bearing more wrapped presents and shouting, "Merry Christmas! Merry Christmas!" Maddened and made insatiable by largesse and lagniappes, the cousins who have been your good and true companions all year, co-authors of endless, creative mischief, will dismiss your doll with a sniff, have a gaudier outfit than yours, give you a frog on your bicep. A warm-up, predinner quarrel will be arbitrated, and you will be sent into the guest bedroom to color in the *Gone With the Wind* coloring book and BE QUIET. You are, for a little while.

Almost certainly there is a piano in some kept-for-company front room, with a bench full of Scotch-taped sheet music and a dead key or two. A cousin known to be musical plays the measured old anthems of Christmas from a *Broadman's Hymnal,* and the family gathers around to sing. An uncle booms out "We Three Kings," the living room fire snickers softly behind its screen, and the fragrance of dinner from the kitchen is frankincense and myrrh.

And finally, after the most spectacular wrapping paper is folded away for next year, the handmade papier-mâché ashtrays admired, the cap pistols taken away, the tearful smallest cousin consoled and his tormentors chastised— Christmas dinner. The dining room table, awkwardly resplendent in company damask and awash in warm fragrances from the kitchen, groans under the ritual feast that never varies. Corn bread dressing. Sweet potatoes with raisins in orange cups, capped with marshmallows. Pickled peaches, cranberry sauce, summer's sweet corn and butter beans from the row of jeweled jars in the cellar. Ambrosia and fruitcake. And, of course, the imperial turkey. No frozen, giant-breasted, butter-basted bird this, but a proper fowl who was alive two days before in a neighbor's barnyard. This is not to be dwelt on, and isn't.

But before the passing around and the clamor for the drumsticks begins, there is the quiet ritual among the tall, flickering Christmas candles of the paying of a debt of gratitude.

Late in the graying afternoon, after naps and mints and a little more coffee and "How about just a little piece of Grace's coconut cake?" a new camera will be brought out, and the Christmas-worn family will be lined up around the already superannuated tree, and another landmark will be inked forever into the map of Christmas country. To become the Christmas the baby was a year old . . . the Christmas Uncle Harvey knocked over the tree . . . the Christmas it snowed . . . the Christmas the children on the McNeil side of the family got German measles . . . the best Christmas, the prettiest tree, the most fun ever.

There are other Christmas countries, as many as there are people for whom there is Christmas. They are better than mine, or worse, or perhaps only very different. They are cities, or they are farms in Nebraska, or they are strip-mining towns in West Virginia, or they really are Jamaica. Or Las Vegas, or somewhere else sun-smitten and stark and wholly unimaginable to me. There are, of course, many Christmas countries that are terrifying howling, empty places. Christmas is a mocking and bitter time to many people; I have friends who truly hate and fear it, and my own Christmases now are brushed, however fleetingly with loss, soiled, and used up after Christmas Day. But I know what it is that I have lost, and these present Christmases don't belong in that other Christmas Country, though these are warm, rich, good holidays, and will undoubtedly be another, a different country, to me one day. Those others belong in childhood, the only one I will ever know, and the only one you will, and that is where I want to go each year.

They are made of garishly sentimental cloth, those places where Christmas is. Part synthetic cloth for many of us. Wholly fabricated for others. But they are as real as the places we live now. Because some small, crying thing in us goes home again for Christmas every year, however briefly and reluctantly, and so for all of us, there is, indeed, a Christmas country.

It is the country of the human heart.

Nature's Celebration

ANNE GRIZZLE, *Texas*

In Houston, the leaves save

their bright red autumn blaze

for the Christ child's celebration,

while others hold tight

to their green to deck the halls.

Christmas in North Carolina

GIGI GRAHAM TCHIVIDJIAN, *NORTH CAROLINA*

Imagine having Billy Graham as the grandfather to your seven children! Enjoy Gigi's candid memory of a typically fun and hectic Graham holiday gathering. L. S. M.

Christmas arrived, with all the joy, excitement, and anticipation that usually accompanies this happy holiday. Our children had been making endless lists for weeks, and each time I was shown another one, I would reply automatically, "Wait until Christmas."

Finally, all was ready, wrapped, and packed for the trip to North Carolina. The closer we got to the mountains and grandparents, the more excited the voices in the car became. The first glimpse of "home," as we drove up the winding drive, and the warm welcome that awaited us—along with homemade apple pie and a cozy fire—all added to our excitement.

This excitement, and the anticipation of all that was yet to come, built to a crescendo on Christmas Eve, as each child (and adult) hung his or her stocking in front of the large fireplace. My daddy gathered all the children around and called Santa at the North Pole—just to make sure he had received all the lists and everything was in order—then wished him a good and speedy trip. Just as the children were all being hurried off to bed, Santa's sleigh bells could be heard above the roof. (They were donkey's bells hung on the chimney and rung by my younger brother at the appropriate moment.) Needless to say, sleep didn't come easily to the children that night.

Christmas morning arrived, and everyone rushed down to the kitchen, dressed in their Sunday best. By tradition, no one is allowed into the living room until all have gathered and finished eating. The children tried to be patient, as the grown-ups slowly drank their coffee and munched their rolls. Just as the last drop of coffee was being downed, my daddy decided it would be better to read the Christmas story before the stockings, instead of later. Amid sighs, he began to read the beautiful story. Even though the children listened, I am afraid they didn't hear much that morning.

Then, to make matters worse, my sister decided pictures should be taken as each child entered the living room, so the children were told to line up and enter one by one. That did it. My eldest son looked up at his grandmother and said in total disgust and exasperation, "Bethlehem was never as miserable as this!"

Christmas Breakfast Casserole

LUCINDA SECREST MCDOWELL, Georgia

Why not start a new family tradition? This one is easy because you prepare it the night before and then just pop in the oven as your family wakes up to Christmas and to the smells of sausage and cheese enticing them down for the celebration. L. S. M.

6 eggs, slightly beaten

2 cups milk

6 slices white bread (trimmed and cubed)

1 cup grated sharp cheddar cheese

1 pound mild bulk sausage

1 teaspoon salt

1 teaspoon dry mustard

Brown sausage and drain. Grease a long casserole dish. Line with cubed bread. Mix together all the other ingredients and pour over bread. Cover tightly and let stand in refrigerator overnight. Bake at 350 degrees for 45 minutes. Serves my family of 6 (probably more if the kids are too excited to eat!).

Trimming the Tree

MARY McDARIES, *Georgia*

My dad, with my elder brother Tom, would go into the forest behind our small home in the hills of Appalachia to look for the biggest and best tree. Meanwhile, the others shelled, cleaned, and popped the popcorn we had grown in the summer just for this occasion. After it was popped, the smaller children were given the duty of stringing the simulated garland.

Then it was time to make the ornaments. Take some flour, yeast, milk, and various food coloring, all in direct proportion to one another. Shape your dough to the desired figure, then paint with food coloring for effect. Stick in the oven until desired hardness. You have made your beautiful tree ornaments without even leaving home.

Then it was time to make the bows. These came from scrap material saved when my mother had made the three girls' dresses over the year. We all helped make the tree-end bows. Finally, after quite a while (Daddy was choosy about our Christmas trees), Daddy and Tom returned with what every year seemed like the best tree ever. Soon, my daddy and all my brothers had the tree stable and standing straight, tall and almost at attention to us kids.

Then it was finally time to decorate the tree.

Being the littlest, I held the popcorn string at the bottom. This brought a great deal of temptation to bite into the string while the others wound it around and up to the top of the tree. Next came our new dough ornaments, along with some that had been saved from Christmases gone by. Then some finishing touches were made, such as our newly finished bows.

The tree trimming was a special part of our Christmas when I was a little girl. It's still special to me today, but back then, it was untainted. Sometimes I wish things could be that simple today.

"What if Christmas were both a
beginning and an end?"

Christmas All the Time

MICHAEL CARD, *Tennessee*

The celebration of the birth of Jesus should be ever new. But for too many of us the scenery of Christmas has become too familiar and comfortable. It blocks our view into the depth of the stark mystery of it all. The mute plastic shepherds cannot speak of awe and worship. The posed porcelain wise men do not remind us of the search for truth. The tinsel star cannot possibly hope to kindle in us the Light that has come blazing into the world.

Perhaps the reason so many of us find it difficult to celebrate the birthday of Jesus is that we have confined the celebration, in many ways, to a single day—and, at that, a day that's become more cluttered than any other day of the year, a day that better represents the noise and business of all our other days. The task, it would seem, is to find afresh the meaning at the heart of Christmas. For when all the trimmings and wrappings are pulled away, the living heart of Christmas is a Child, a Man, a King, and we must discover, most of all, what He means.

What if Christmas day were both a beginning and an end? The beginning of a celebration of Jesus that would not end until the next Christmas, when it would begin all over again?

What if the wisemen's worship and the shepherds' awe became, if not a daily then at least a weekly occurrence for us?

What if the peace and rest of the nativity became a part of every day?

What if Christmas were no longer a "holiday," but a holy day, infusing all our days with holiness?

These are the questions, the hopes I bring to the sights so familiar in my own mind—the star, the stable, and all the assembled company of witnesses in the skies and on the earth. I feel a deep need to ask of them: What is the meaning of this event? What promise lies here? As we begin, I confess I don't know what answers the Lord might give. I approach, armed only with the conviction that He is the Answer. And though He seems to give direct "answers" sparingly, He would not leave us without an answer to our important questions.

Where are you, Lord Jesus? Is seeing your face as simple as gazing down into a manger's hay? Is there a deserted stable somewhere, aglow with your Presence? Might I join a band of magi and follow a star to you? Might I keep watch with simple shepherds and bear the good news from Gabriel's own luminous lips?

Where are you, O Lord? Grant me the grace to find you again. Give me ears to hear angel words that whisper every day of you. Give me eyes to see the dim stable-lit truth of your Incarnation every night.

Give me strength to follow, 364 days, whatever star might lead me to you on the 365th. That some day I might behold, unsquinting, the radiance of your Glory in a season that will be forever!

Go Tell It on the Mountain

Some consider this spiritual, created late in the nineteenth century, as one of the very finest carols ever conceived. It is probably anonymous, but may possibly have been the work of Frederick J. Work, an African-American Nashville-born composer. L. S. M.

While shepherds kept their watching
O'er silent flocks by night,
Behold throughout the heavens,
There shone a holy light.

> *Go tell it on the mountain,*
> *Over the hills and everywhere;*
> *Go tell it on the mountain*
> *That Jesus Christ is born!*

The shepherds feared and trembled
When lo! above the earth
Rang out the angel chorus
That hailed our Savior's birth.

Go tell it on the mountain,
Over the hills and everywhere;
Go tell it on the mountain
That Jesus Christ is born!

Down in a lowly manger
Our humble Christ was born,
And God sent us salvation
That blessed Christmas morn.

> *Go tell it on the mountain,*
> *Over the hills and everywhere;*
> *Go tell it on the mountain*
> *That Jesus Christ is born!*

The Lost Christmas

CELESTINE SIBLEY, *Georgia*

*I first read this story when I was ten years old, just like Sandra.
It made such an impact on my view of Christmas that I read it
again every year to remember the true meaning of Christmas—
"It's the loving and the giving that count!"* L. S. M.

Chapter 1

Sandra Dunstan looked around to make sure nobody was watching her, then she carefully poured her milk into the guppy tank. The milk mushroomed slowly downward, leaving a widening cloudy trail that blotted out the tiny fish, the feathery water plants, and the little stone castle in the sand on the bottom of the tank.

Sandra, who was ten and should have known better, shook her soft blond hair out of her face and giggled softly.

She heard a noise behind her and spun around guiltily. Her older brother, Michael, who was twelve, had come into the breakfast room and was looking at the aquarium with interest.

"Save the women and children first!" he called out suddenly. He picked up a piece of toast and threw it into the tank.

"Oh, Mike, what fun!" cried Sandra. "Let's give them some oars. How about bacon?" She grabbed two pieces of bacon off a plate on the table and crisscrossed it on the toast.

"They need provisions, too," said Mike. "A shipwreck kit. Put in a little cereal."

Sandra threw him a delighted smile and picked up a bowl of oatmeal. "A spoonful for each guppy," she said, ladling it generously onto the soggy toast, which promptly sank from the weight.

"Too bad," sympathized Michael. "We'll have to launch another life raft. Here." He set another piece of toast afloat on the surface of the water.

"How about a grapefruit boat?" inquired Sandra. "Rub-a-dub-dub, three men in a tub!"

"Swell," cried Michael, throwing half a grapefruit into the tank with such vigor the cloudy, fish-smelling water splashed all over the floor.

"Quick, we need oil to pour on troubled waters," Sandra said and turned from the table to the sideboard where the cruet holding the vinegar and oil customarily sat.

At that moment Mrs. Hoyt, their father's housekeeper, walked into the breakfast room.

"Children!" she cried. "What are you doing to the poor fish? Quick, get them out of that slop!"

Michael looked from the plump gray-haired woman, whose always pink face was now red from annoyance and distress, to the puddles on the waxed floor. He smiled.

"Show us, Mrs. Hoyt," he invited. And then so softly only Sandra could hear it, he added, "Show us, as Hansel said to the old witch."

The words were no sooner out of his mouth than Mrs. Hoyt walked toward the guppy tank, her feet met the puddle on the floor, and she lurched and slid and sprawled flat on her back on the breakfast room floor.

Both children doubled up with laughter.

"Mrs. Hoyt, you're so funny!" cried Sandra. "You look positively cute!"

And Michael, who had anticipated the housekeeper's accident, was speechless with merriment.

That was the scene which met Mr. Daniel Dunstan's eyes on a December morning a few days before

Christmas when he came down to breakfast in his home on Peachtree Road.

His housekeeper floundered awkwardly on the floor, the guppies rose to the top of the tide of garbage in their aquarium and gasped their last. And his beloved son and daughter, who were, as he well knew, responsible for the whole mess, clutched their sides and laughed uproariously.

Dan Dunstan was a patient man, lonely since the death of his wife five years before, and normally soft-spoken. But that morning he let out a roar that caused his comfortable, handsome home to rock on its foundations.

"Shut up, you little monsters!" he yelled at his children as he hurried to help Mrs. Hoyt to her feet. "Shut up and get the mop!"

Now nobody had ever told Sandra or Michael Dunstan to get a mop before—and, odd as it may seem, that was really the beginning of the most remarkable Christmas they ever spent. That was the first step in the strange Christmas adventure of two of the most spoiled children who ever lived in Atlanta, Georgia, or elsewhere.

Chapter 2

If ever two children needed Christmas, it was Sandra and Michael Dunstan. They needed it worse than Mrs. Hoyt thought they needed a spanking. They needed it worse than their exhausted and exasperated teachers thought they needed to be taken out of their elegant private school and committed to the state training schools for delinquents. Even their psychiatrist didn't really know how much Sandra and

Michael had lived without really knowing about Christmas.

Only their father, tired and rich and sometimes awfully lonely, suspected the sad little secret about his children. Because their mother was dead, he had tried to give them everything he could think of that children needed, including the most lavish Christmases money could buy.

Yet that December morning when they wasted their food and killed the guppies and stood by laughing while Mrs. Hoyt skidded and fell on the floor in the mess they had made, Mr. Dunstan realized that Sandra and Michael were ignorant, underprivileged little children.

"Did you realize that Mrs. Hoyt might have hurt herself?" he asked them after the housekeeper had limped out and they had sat down once more to a fresh breakfast.

Michael looked bland and innocent.

"Oh, no, sir," he lied.

"How about your fish," the father asked. "Did you intend to kill them?"

Sandra and Michael exchanged pained looks and Sandra rolled her eyes heavenward with a show of great boredom. Michael sighed heavily and pushed his untouched food away. They hated lectures and they planned not to listen if they could help it.

"I'm really surprised that you should behave so badly so close to Christmas," Mr. Dunstan went on.

Sandra laughed scornfully.

"You mean we won't get any presents?" she said. "Well, okay, don't give us any presents."

"There's nothing I want particularly anyhow," said Michael indifferently. "I've got a lot of junk you can have back if you want it."

Mr. Dunstan sat quietly a moment looking at his children—Sandra, a delicate little blond girl so like her beautiful mother, and Michael, strong and sturdy with bright close-cropped brown hair and fine blue eyes. They were handsome children and he loved them, but they weren't any comfort or pleasure to him and he couldn't understand why.

He sighed heavily.

"I wasn't thinking of presents," he said. "There's something more to Christmas than that. I guess it's my fault you don't know. I tell you what . . ." His eyes brightened and he looked at them hopefully. "How would you all like to go away with me for a few days—just the three of us?"

"Where?" said Sandra. "California? I'd love to see the movie stars."

"Oh, California," sneered Michael. "Let's go some place decent for a change. I'd like a little excitement."

Mr. Dunstan looked at them sadly.

"I think we'll try the North Georgia mountains," he said. "One of the men at the office has a shack up there I think I can borrow. It's primitive. We'll have to do our own cooking and probably cut wood and haul water, but it's very quiet and we'll have wonderful walks and talks."

"Oh, great," commented Sandra bitterly.

"*Some* Christmas," muttered Michael. "Of all the corny things to do!"

Chapter 3

Sandra didn't have any idea how long she had been riding when the headlights of the car picked up a little side road and her father slowed down and stopped. She was on the back seat with the boxes of groceries and covers and Michael was slumped down on the front seat, pretending to sleep because he had run out of sulky answers to his father's conversation.

"This must be the place," said Mr. Dunstan cheerfully. "There's the big white pine tree with the lightning blaze on its face, and there's the little creek. We've come about eight miles since we left the pavement—and that's where Sam said we'd turn off."

He maneuvered the car into the little side road and started moving slowly down a bank toward a creek.

"And there's the house," he said triumphantly. "This is the place."

"Where's the house?" asked Michael, peering into the woods.

"There," said Mr. Dunstan. "Two rooms and a screened porch. That's what Sam said."

"Call that a house?" said Sandra petulantly from the back seat. "Looks like a little shack to me."

"Dump," said Michael briefly.

Mr. Dunstan said nothing but concentrated on fording the creek and getting up the small hill beside the house. He parked the car and got out with his flashlight and keys to try the door. The door swung open and he turned to the car and called, "This is it, kids. Hop out and let's get unpacked."

"I don't feel so good," said Michael. "My side hurts again."

"Have we got to stay here?" inquired Sandra. "I'm so co-old and it looks so dark and scary. Can't we go back to a motel, Daddy?"

Mr. Dunstan opened the door and began pulling boxes and bundles out. "Let's give it a try, children," he said. "Come on. We'll build a fire and have the cabin warm in no time at all. I know you're hungry. Mrs. Hoyt packed us a nice lunch and there's a bottle of cocoa back here somewhere. Give me a hand."

Michael and Sandra climbed reluctantly out of the car and stood looking about them. The December moon was big and it threw a frosty light on the little cabin and the stiff winter grass. Somewhere behind them in the shadows they heard the icy tinkle of the creek. It sounded cold and lonesome, and they hurried after their father into the cabin.

The beam of his flashlight showed a long, plain room with bunk beds in the corners and a big stone fireplace in the center. He found a kerosene lamp and lit it and then knelt by the hearth and began building a fire from the dry wood he found in the box by the chimney.

The flames leaped up and he hoisted a big gray log in place. Turning from the hearth, he rubbed his hands together and faced his son and daughter, smiling.

"Poor babies," he said, reaching out a hand to draw each of them close to him. "You're tired and cold and sleepy. Sit here and warm up and I'll bring in the rest of our things and we'll eat something and go to bed. Tomorrow we're going to have a fine time. First thing in the morning I'm going to show you how to make the best flapjacks you ever put in your mouth."

"Ugh!" said Sandra, shrugging off her father's arm.

But Michael waited until their father had gone back out to the car again before he said anything. Then he said softly but determinedly, "Tomorrow, Sandy, we're going to run away."

Chapter 4

The morning was bright blue and silver—blue sky and frost-silvered earth with the bare branches of the trees making a delicate tracery of charcoal shadows against both earth and sky. But Sandra and Michael were too busy running away to notice that.

They left the little cabin before breakfast, when the ring of an axe on the wooded slope back of the cabin told them their father was where he would not see them.

Now it was midmorning and the air in the North Georgia mountains was sharp and sparkling as a cut-glass goblet—and Sandra and Michael were hopelessly lost.

"My side hurts," said Michael, stumbling up a rocky slope.

"Oh, your side!" scoffed Sandra. "You're all the time using your side since you had your appendix out. Use it on Daddy and Mrs. Hoyt but don't tell me it hurts. I know better. You got us lost and a hurting side's not going to find us."

"Aw shut up," said Michael but without much heat.

He was hungry and worried. Somehow his sense of direction was off. It had been his plan to take a shortcut through the woods to the highway, where he knew he and his sister could hitchhike back to their home in Atlanta. That, he felt, would show their father that they did not intend to be pushed into spending Christmas in an isolated mountain cabin and listen to his lectures.

He smirked a little, thinking how even now Daddy would be searching for them and worrying, maybe even cursing himself, Michael thought hopefully, for bringing his children to such a place.

He stepped on a loose rock and his feet slipped out from under him, sending him sprawling among the rocks and briars. Sandra began giggling, but a long thorny branch snapped back and hit her in the face, scratching her nose and drawing blood from her cheek. She cried instead.

Michael sat up and caressed his bruised ankle with his hand. There was a time when he would have laughed at Sandra's tears, but something—maybe his hurting leg or being hungry and lost—made him feel sorry for her.

"I tell you what, Sandy," he said gruffly. "Let's go back to the cabin where Daddy is. We probably got him worried enough. And we could get something to eat."

"Yes," said Sandra, gulping a little and wiping her eyes. "He was going to make flapjacks. But are you sure you know the way back?"

"Sure," said Michael getting to his feet. "We'll get back on that little creek and just follow it."

Sandra wiped her cheek where the salt of a tear caused the briar scratch to smart and smiled at her brother in real admiration.

"Let's go," she said.

They did go, slowly and painfully, with more briar scratches on their faces and arms and occasional falls where footing was tricky. They found a creek, and began following it. A dun-colored cloud floated lazily off the top of a mountain and hung itself over the sun, turning the day from blue and silver to dull gray. They got their shoes wet in the marshy places along the creek and their feet grew stiff and ached with cold. Michael lost his cap and Sandra lost one of her bright red mittens.

The creek bank was a tangle of vines and dark green clumps of mountain laurel and rhododendron, so dim and jungle-like in places, the children didn't realize for a time that it was growing dark.

When they came to a clearing and saw the light had gone from the sky, Sandra began to cry.

"Hush, Sandy," said Michael desperately. "Hush. I think I hear something."

And miraculously enough, when Sandra stopped crying he did hear something. He heard a whistled tune and the tune was the sweetest of all Christmas melodies—"Silent Night, Holy Night."

Just then as he and Sandra stared into the gathering darkness, they saw the tune came with a boy—a boy who was driving a cow along a path at the edge of the clearing.

Chapter 5

Sandra and Michael thought they had never seen a prettier sight in their lives than the house to which Pete Mills and his cow, Fancy, led them that cold December evening.

It was a humpbacked little house nudged up against a mountainside for warmth. It had no paint on its walls but a tendril of blue smoke from the chimney was busy skywriting a welcome over its roof. And its doorway, standing open, was a bright square of firelight.

They stood by the fireplace and felt the warmth of the flames steal achingly over their numb hands and feet while the voice of Pete's mother, who sat in a chair in the corner, warmed them with its welcome. Her face was thin and pale but her voice was strong and hearty.

"Young'uns, git to stirring," she called out to the four little girls, all younger than Pete, who made a circle about Sandra and Michael and stood smiling shyly.

"We got company—Christmas company! You know how that banty rooster has been crowing all day. I told you company was coming and here it is! Ivy, set places at the table. Maybeth, warm up the leather britches and the crackling bread. Pete, hurry with the milking. Warm milk will taste good on a night like this!"

The children scattered as she spoke, throwing Michael and Sandra radiant smiles.

"Now!" said the mother. "Give the least ones your jackets to hang up, and pull up chairs. We're the Millses. Them least ones is our twins, Katie and Laurie. They're little but the most help to me. Hand 'em your coats."

Shyly Sandra and Michael complied. Then Michael, because he was the oldest, gravely took upon himself the responsibility of an explanation.

"We're the Dunstans," he said. "I'm Michael, she's Sandra. We live in Atlanta but we were up at Mr.

Sam Jackson's cabin with our father and we . . . we got lost."

"Lost?" said Mrs. Mills. "Mercy! Is your father lost too?"

"We don't know," faltered Sandra, suddenly thinking of her father, who might be wandering through the dark woods, looking for them. "We left him at the cabin." She looked anxiously at Michael. She didn't want to tell this nice, welcoming woman they had run away.

"Then you'uns is all right," said Mrs. Mills, relieved. "He'll find you. I don't know where that there cabin you're talking about is. We seldom git over yon mountain. But you'uns stay put and your folks'll find you."

She laughed. "Like I tell my chaps, a lost bairn is a heap easier to find than a lost calf. Bairns rare back in a clearing and stay still but calves git the go-yonders."

Her tone was so merry, Michael and Sandra laughed in spite of their weariness and their hunger.

"We'll make like a barn," offered Michael sturdily.

"Yes, do that," said Mrs. Mills. And then in a more serious tone she beckoned them closer to her chair. "I been sitting here praying the Lord would send the young'uns something fine and special for Christmas," she whispered. "I think you'uns come a-purpose to answer that prayer. I couldn't be prouder to see anybody."

Sandra and Michael looked at each other uncomfortably.

"We haven't got any presents," Sandra said apologetically.

"Presents!" cried Mrs. Mills. "Lord love you, we don't want presents. You brought yourselves. And hit's Christmas Eve. After you've et and rested we'll have ourselves a Christmas party!"

The leather britches—tender green beans which were snapped and threaded on strings and hung in the rafters to dry until they were pale gold—had been boiled with bacon rinds and a pod of red pepper, and they tasted of sun and summertime. The crackling bread had been cooked in a pone so it was crisp outside but rich and moist with bits of lean pork inside. The milk, foaming and warm from the cow, Fancy, tasted so good Michael and Sandra could scarcely believe it was the same stuff they had poured in the guppy tank.

They ate, and as they ate the young Millses stood watching them happily.

"When you'uns done eating," said Pete, "reckon you'll feel like coming out to the barn and he'p us with our surprise?"

Michael and Sandra answered the question in one breath.

"Sure!" they said.

Chapter 6

The twins, Katie and Laurie, stayed by the fireside with their mother, but Ivy and Maybeth and Pete led the Dunstan children to the barn, shepherding them along in the light of the kerosene lantern.

"Hit's a Christmas tree we got," lithe dark-eyed Maybeth confided to Sandra in a whisper. "Have you'uns got a Christmas tree at your home?"

"Yes," said Sandra, thinking of the tall blue spruce which stood in the living room at home, decked with its strings of electric lights and glittering ornaments and scarcely noticed by Sandra and Mike in their boredom with Christmas.

"Oh, I know hit's a pretty one," said Maybeth politely. And Ivy, who was ten, smiled over her younger sister's head at Sandra.

"Wait till you see our'n," she said. "Maybeth's put the prettiest decorations of all on it."

Pete swung the barn door open and Michael and Sandra looked at the tree and swallowed miserably.

It was a little tree, straight and symmetrical, with its roots carefully packed in earth in a wooden bucket, but not a light did it have on it, not a glittering ornament, not a piece of tinsel, not a candy cane.

Paper chains cut out of the colored pages of the mail-order catalogue were draped over its branches. But the other things on it certainly were not colorful. In fact, they were almost indistinguishable in the lantern light.

"It's pretty," offered Sandra at last.

"Oh, hit ain't much to look at," said Pete offhandedly. "Hit's a smell and taste and feel tree. For Ma."

"For your mother?" said Michael, surprised.

"Ma's blind," said Pete quietly.

"Blind!" The Dunstans said the word together and then stared at Pete in horror and disbelief.

He smiled serenely. "Ma can see things a lot of folks can't see, but she can't see a Christmas tree. And she loves Christmas better than any time. We put the tree in a bucket so it would live and stay green and smell good, and then we gathered up the presents she could smell and taste and feel. See?"

He drew Michael and Sandra closer to examine the little bunches of dried, sweet-smelling herbs Maybeth had tied to the branches, the bright chain of hot peppers from Ivy, the little bird's nest Pete himself had found last summer and saved.

There were packets of flower seeds from the twins and a bag of black walnuts they had picked up on the mountainside. Pete had put two arrowheads on a branch next to the base of the tree.

"Watch Ma when her fingers touch 'em," he exulted. "She'll know right off they're arryheads and she'll hold them in the palm of her hand and tell stories about the Cherokee Indians that used to live in these mountains and hunt with them things instead of bullets. Ma knows a heap of stories."

"What about the children?" asked Sandra anxiously. "Don't children get presents too?"

"Sure," said Pete sturdily. "Ma's got dolls hid away for the twins. Ivy and Maybeth had boughten dolls when our daddy was a-living, and they give 'em to Ma to dress up all new for the least ones."

"Oh, I wish I could give your mother a present!" Sandra said suddenly. And she didn't realize it was the first time in her life she had ever wanted to give anybody a present.

"Me, too," said Michael unexpectedly.

Pete and Ivy and Maybeth looked at them attentively. Finally Pete said to Michael, "Can you read?"

"Of course," said Michael, mystified.

"Good?" put in Ivy.

"Why, yes, I think so," said Michael.

The three Mills children exchanged delighted looks.

"Then you can read to Ma," said Pete. "We'll take the tree to the fire and have the party. And you can read Ma the Christmas story out of the Bible. She purely loves to hear it."

Michael grabbed hold of the bucket bearing the little tree and marched ahead, holding it triumphantly aloft. Sandra had to run to catch up with them but she grabbed Pete's sleeve at the steps.

"I . . . I could sing," she offered breathlessly. "I could sing your mother a song."

Pete's eyes on her were bright with approval and gratitude.

"Why, that'll be a fine present," he said. "Fine as silk."

Chapter 7

All the rest of the Christmases they lived Sandra and Michael were to remember that Christmas Eve in a little house in the North Georgia hills.

When they had helped the Mills children haul their "smell-taste-feel" tree in to the fireside, they placed it before the chair of the bright-faced blind woman who sat there. Then they all gathered at Mrs. Mills's feet on the floor for the presents.

Michael gave his present first—the Bible reading. Proudly little Maybeth brought him the worn family Bible and all their faces turned toward him, waiting expectantly. He had trouble finding the place in the Bible and his hands trembled and his voice quavered a little as he started, but as he read his voice gathered strength.

And the radiance on the face of the blind woman and the eager hush in the little room made the words seem to sing as he read them out:

"And, lo, the angel of the Lord came upon them, and the glory of the Lord shone round about them: and they were sore afraid. And the angel said unto them, 'Fear not: for, behold, I bring you good tidings of great joy, which shall be to all people.' "

"You see, children," said Mrs. Mills reverently, "that's the way it was. Oh, it was a wondrous thing the way we come to have Christmas! How could a body ever feel any way but happy knowing how He come into the world, the pore little mite of a thing!"

The children listened, and she talked over the details of the Baby's birth, making it seem as real to them as the firelight about them. It was to her a most loved story and she savored the words as she spoke them, pausing now and then to shake her head and smile at the wonder of it all.

Then she reached out her hands, the sensitive, seeking, work-worn hands of a poor blind woman, and Sandra watched them move over the plain lithe, grand little tree. They touched every gift upon it with so much love. Sandra looked quickly at Michael to see if he noticed too.

Love, she thought, that's what Daddy was trying to tell us about Christmas. It's the loving and the giving that count. Not the presents, either poor ones or rich ones.

Pete brought a bottle of sweet apple cider out of the fruit house and Ivy fetched gingerbread from the kitchen. Sandra, who could tell from the solemn face on Michael that he was thinking of Daddy and wanted to see him too, put an arm around each of the twins and started singing. She sang all the Christmas carols she knew—the ones she had scorned in school and the ones she pretended not to know in church.

And then patiently she went back over the words and taught them to the Mills children.

The firelight hardly showed at all outside the house when the door was closed, so it must have been the sound of their voices lifted joyfully in the song "Angels, from the Realms of Glory" that guided Mr. Dunstan and his search party to the door.

And the welcome he got when Sandra and Michael heard his loud "Hello!" outside! They went tumbling out the door to meet him and drag him to the fire, hugging him and laughing and crying in a way the poor bewildered man hardly understood at all. If he had intended to punish them for running away, he changed his mind. But that may have been because he saw something different in them.

When they rode down the mountain together in the back of the forest ranger's jeep, they leaned against their father and looked at the big bright star in the east. It seemed very close and bright and Sandra thought she knew what Mrs. Mills would say about it.

"That star," she murmured to her father, "has the most important story to tell."

Mr. Dunstan smiled and held them close. He knew all along the Christmas story is a love story.

There Will Be Less Someday

RUTH BELL GRAHAM, *North Carolina*

There will be less someday—
much less,
and there will be More:
less to distract
and amuse;
More, to adore;
less to burden
and confuse;
More, to undo
the cluttering of centuries,
that we might view
again, That which star
and angels
pointed to;
we shall be poorer—
and richer;
stripped—and free:
for always there will be a Gift,
always
a Tree!

Christmas Night

MAX LUCADO, *Texas*

It's Christmas night. The house is quiet. Even the crackle is gone from the fireplace. Warm coals issue a lighthouse glow in the darkened den. Stockings hang empty on the mantle. The tree stands naked in the corner. Christmas cards, tinsel, and memories remind Christmas night of Christmas day.

It's Christmas night. What a day it has been! Spiced tea. Santa Claus. Cranberry sauce. "Thank you so much." "You shouldn't have!" "Grandma is on the phone." Knee-deep wrapping paper. "It just fits." Flashing cameras.

It's Christmas night. The girls are in bed. Jenna dreams of her talking Big Bird and clutches her new purse. Andrea sleeps in her new Santa pajamas.

It's Christmas night. The tree that only yesterday grew from soil made of gifts, again grows from the Christmas tree stand. Presents are now possessions. Wrapping paper is bagged and in the dumpster. The dishes are washed and leftover turkey awaits next week's sandwiches.

It's Christmas night. The last of the carolers appeared on the ten o'clock news. The last of the apple pie was eaten by my brother-in-law. And the last of the Christmas albums have been stored away, having dutifully performed their annual rendition of chestnuts, white Christmases, and red-nosed reindeer.

It's Christmas night.

The midnight hour has chimed and I should be asleep, but I'm awake. I'm kept awake by one stunning thought. The world was different this week. It was temporarily transformed.

The magical dust of Christmas glittered on the cheeks of humanity ever so briefly, reminding us of what is worth having and what we were intended to be. We forgot our compulsion with winning, wooing, and warring. We put away our ladders and ledgers, we hung up our stopwatches and weapons. We stepped off our racetracks and roller coasters and looked outward toward the star of Bethlehem.

It's the season to be jolly because, more than at any other time, we think of him. More than in any other season, his name is on our lips.

And the result? For a few precious hours our heavenly yearnings intermesh, and we become a chorus. A ragtag chorus of longshoremen, Boston lawyers, illegal immigrants, housewives, and a thousand other peculiar persons who are banking that Bethlehem's mystery is in reality, a reality. "Come and behold him" we sing, stirring even the sleepiest of shepherds and pointing them toward the Christ child.

For a few precious hours, he is beheld. Christ the Lord. Those who pass the year without seeing him, suddenly see him. People who have been accustomed to using his name in vain, pause to use it in praise. Eyes, now free of the blinders of self, marvel at his majesty.

All of a sudden he's everywhere.

In the grin of the policeman as he drives the paddy wagon full of presents to the orphanage.

In the twinkle in the eyes of the Taiwanese waiter as he tells of his upcoming Christmas trip to see his children.

In the emotion of the father who is too thankful to finish the dinner table prayer.

He's in the tears of the mother as she welcomes home her son from overseas.

He's in the heart of the man who spent Christmas morning on skid row giving away cold baloney sandwiches and warm wishes.

And he's in the solemn silence of the crowd of shopping mall shoppers as the elementary school chorus sings "Away in a Manger."

Emmanuel. He is with us. God came near.

It's Christmas night. In a few hours the clean-up will begin—lights will come down, trees will be thrown out. Size 36 will be exchanged for size 40, eggnog will be on sale for half price. Soon life will be normal again. December's generosity will become January's payments, and the magic will begin to fade.

But for the moment, the magic is still in the air. Maybe that's why I'm still awake. I want to savor the spirit just a bit more. I want to pray that those who beheld him today will look for him next August. And I can't help but linger on one fanciful thought: If he can do so much with such timid prayers lamely offered in December, how much more could he do if we thought of him every day?

Acknowledgments

Grateful acknowledgment is made to the following for permission to use their material:

"Appalachian Christmas" by Lyndall Toothman is taken from *A Foxfire Christmas*, Wigginton, E., ed., pp. 86, 91-92. Published by the Foxfire Fund, Inc., Mountain City, GA. © 1989. Reprinted by permission.

"Blue Jeans and Jesus" © 1998 by Sharron M. McDonald first appeared in *Virtue* magazine, Dec. 1998/Jan. 1999, a publication of Christianity Today, Inc. Used by permission of author.

"Christmas All the Time" © 1991 by Michael Card is taken from *The Promise: A Celebration of Christ's Birth*. Used by permission of author and Michael Card Music, Franklin, TN. International copyright secured. All rights reserved.

"Christmas Country" © 1964 by Anne Rivers Siddons is taken from *John Chancellor Makes Me Cry* (Garden City, NY: Doubleday, 1975). Originally titled "A Southern Christmas," it was first published in *Atlanta Magazine*, December 1964. Used by permission of author. All rights reserved.

"Christmas Night" by Max Lucado is taken from *God Came Near*,© 1987 by Max Lucado. Used by permission of Multnomah Publishers, Inc., Sisters, OR.

"Christmas in North Carolina" © 1981 by Gigi Tchividjian. Originally published in *A Woman's Quest for Serenity* (Grand Rapids, MI.: Fleming Revell, 1981). Used by permission of author. All rights reserved.

"Christmas in the South" © 1999 by Lucinda Secrest McDowell. Used by permission of author. All rights reserved.

"A Christmas Verse" © 1997 by Pratt Secrest. First published in *For Better . . . For Verse*, © 1999 by Pratt Secrest. Used by permission of author.

"Creating Christmas Memories" © 1999 by Lucinda Secrest McDowell. Used by permission of author. All rights reserved.

"Flora Mae's Biscuits" taken from *Born in the Kitchen*, ©1979 by Flora Mae Hunter. Pinecone Press, Tallahassee, FL.

"A Fresh Approach to the Holidays" by Ann Hibbard is taken from *Family Celebrations at Christmas*, © 1988, 1993 by Ann Hibbard. A Raven's Ridge Book. Used by permission of Baker Book House, Grand Rapids, MI.

"Handel's Gift" as told by Evelyn Pratt Secrest. This edited version © 2000 by Lucinda Secrest McDowell. Used by permission of author's family.

"How to Keep Your Christmas Joy" by Charles L. Allen is excerpted from *Christmas in Our Hearts* by Charles L. Allen and Charles L. Wallis, © 1957 by Fleming H. Revell, a division of Baker Book House, Grand Rapids, MI. Used by permission.